BUSINESS FORMS MANAGEMENT

BUSINESS FORMS MANAGEMENT

WILLIAM V. NYGREN

amacom

A Division of American Management Associations

Library of Congress Cataloging in Publication Data

Nygren, William V.
 Business forms management.

 Includes index.
 1. Business—Forms, blanks, etc. 2. Management.
I. Title.
HF5317.N94   651′.29   79-54845
ISBN 0-8144-5524-7

First Printing

THIS book is dedicated to the thousands of people
already using forms management principles
to improve the effectiveness and efficiency
of their organizations.

PREFACE

"Somebody has to do something about all this paperwork!"

I've heard this many times, from people at all job levels, in many organizations. It seems to be a universal feeling that today's paperwork systems are a problem. People recognize that forms and procedures desperately need review and improvement.

Yet, at the same time, I hear forms managers, analysts, and designers complain about the lack of recognition they receive from their organizations, about the resistance to their services, about the people who bypass them at every opportunity. Unfortunately, this, too, seems to be universal.

Those in forms administration should ask, "What is there about my forms function that turns people off? Why don't they want what I have to offer? What's wrong?" Maybe the service is too slow or of poor quality. Maybe the attitude displayed is inappropriate or the objectives of the helper are different from those of the one needing help. Many causes of dissatisfaction could create the resistance so often experienced.

On the other hand, people using the services of a forms function should acquire a better understanding of the benefits available and their importance.

This book, written from what I've learned from my experiences as a forms administrator at 3M Company and from conducting many seminars for the American Management Associations, Business Forms Management Association, and other organizations, is designed to help fulfill these needs. With proper attitudes, the right objectives, good understanding, efficient operating procedures, and cooperation from the rest of the organization, forms administration programs can be effective tools of modern management. They can help increase the productivity and profitability of any organization.

No book of this type is the result of just one person's efforts. While I accept responsibility for all of the information, it is obviously not all new. The concepts and practices discussed were developed over a period of years by reading previously published material, especially that written by Frank Knox, Ray Marien, Les Matthies, Belden Menkus, and Carl Osteen; and by interacting with co-workers at 3M and with forms management personnel from other firms.

I also acknowledge and appreciate AMACOM's editorial assistance in converting the original draft into this final product.

Finally, I would like to thank my wife and children for their support and understanding during the many evening, weekend, and vacation hours invested in this effort.

William V. Nygren

CONTENTS

1

Introduction

EVERY function in every organization should have a reason for existence. Forms administration is no exception to this commonsense rule. Because it is an emerging field, forms administration is scrutinized more closely than other functions of an organization. It does not have the inertia of historical precedent—the "everybody does it this way" attitude toward it—that long-established functions have.

As more and more managers look at forms administration, they are recognizing the need to improve the way their paperwork is processed, and the role that forms administration can play in this improvement effort. They have found that a forms administration function can save the organization more money than it costs to operate.

One day through the primeval wood
A calf walked home as good calves should;
But left a trail all bent askew,
A crooked trail as calves all do.

A dog took up the trail next day
A bear, too, went along that way.
And then a wise bellwether sheep
Pursued the trail o'er vale and steep.

And drew his flock behind him too
As good bellwethers always do.
And from that day, o'er hill and glade
Through those old woods a path was made.

And many men wound in and out
And dodged and turned and bent about.
And uttered words of righteous wrath
Because 'twas such a crooked path.

The forest path became a lane
That bent and turned and bent again.
And this, before men were aware,
Became a city's thoroughfare.

And soon the central street was this
of a renowned metropolis.
A hundred thousand men were led
By one calf, near three centuries dead.

For men are prone to go it blind
Along the calf paths of the mind
And work away from sun to sun
To do what other men have done.

They keep the path a sacred groove
Along which all their lives they move;
But how the wise old wood gods laugh
who saw that first primeval calf!

This poem, written in 1895, describes the way in which many of our procedures, policies, reports, and forms have been developed. Every form was created to meet a need. They've all been added to or changed, but very few have ever been eliminated. Most forms are used now because they are part of the routine, even though the original need for the information may no longer exist.

As the poem about the calf indicates, we all have a tendency to continue acting in a habitual pattern. This can be good and efficient, as long as those actions are beneficial. In a work situation, this means they should be *productive* and *effective*.

Most business leaders study closely the work habits and patterns of production workers. They are very concerned over the cost per unit produced, because they know that production costs have a direct effect on profits. They see the value of spending time and money to help production workers do their jobs in the most effective manner possible. And, partly as a result of these concerns, the productivity of production workers has increased 90 percent during the last ten years, while white-collar productivity has risen only 4 percent.*

* Jay Timmons, "Increasing the efficiency of office workers as a means to halt inflation," *The Office* (July 1979), pp. 124–125.

2

Because it is so difficult to measure administrative efforts, concern over the productivity of clerical staffs is much less specific. Many managers are unaware of the effect that clerical productivity can have on an organization's profits.

PAPERWORK AND PRODUCTIVITY

How Much Paperwork Do We Do?

According to a 1968 survey of American business, about 40 percent of all working hours are spent doing clerical work. Three-fourths of that time, or 30 percent of all hours, is spent processing forms or reports in some manner. If we apply a conservative $12,000-per-year salary cost to these percentages, we estimate that:

- A firm with 500 employees spends about $1,800,000 per year processing forms and reports
- A 5,000-employee firm spends $18,000,000 annually
- A 50,000-employee organization spends about $180,000,000 per year on paperwork processing

What does your organization spend each year to process paperwork? Figure it out. Based on this survey, it would be about 30 percent of your payroll cost. In many paper-oriented organizations, such as banks, insurance companies, government agencies, much more than the average amount of time will be spent processing forms.

Other indications of the amount of paperwork are the number of different forms being used and the total amount of paper used in those forms. I have heard it said that the average company spends about $125 per year for forms for each employee on the payroll. Based on this estimate,

- The 500-employee firm uses about $62,500 worth of forms each year
- The 5,000-employee firm uses about $625,000 worth of forms per year
- The 50,000-employee organization spends about $6,250,000 per year on forms

3

It is not unusual for a large firm to have well over 10,000 different forms in use, with a total usage of several hundred million sheets of paper each year.

These estimates do not necessarily reflect a *bad* situation. The number of forms used, the volume of paper consumed, and the time taken to process the forms demonstrate the fact that paperwork processing is a very major part of our business operations. In a private business, paperwork processing has a big effect on profits. In government, it has a significant effect on the tax dollars needed to perform a necessary service.

How Well Do We Do Our Paperwork?

According to a survey conducted in 1968, in the average business about 28 percent of the time spent processing paperwork is wasted because of inefficient forms and procedures. This means:

- The 500-employee firm is wasting $504,000 per year because of paperwork inefficiencies
- The 5,000-employee firm is wasting $5,040,000 per year
- The 50,000-employee organization is wasting $50,400,000 per year

These figures are an indictment of management. How much does your organization waste each year because of inefficient forms and procedures? According to this study, it is about 8.4 percent of your total payroll costs.

Methods for Improving Paperwork

Unfortunately, some managers have the mistaken idea that things left alone will tend to correct themselves, that some natural process will rectify the situation. But this problem simply will not go away by itself. Other managers recognize that inefficiencies exist, and order across-the-board personnel reductions or hiring restrictions in an attempt to solve the problem. This approach has a detrimental effect on employee morale, especially among the most effective managers. Employees and outsiders conclude that top executives have let an unsatisfactory management situation become a crisis. If more prudent action had been taken earlier, as part of a normal activity, the "crisis" could have been avoided.

A third type of reaction to ineffectiveness is a "get-tough" policy. This comes from those who believe that all employees are naturally lazy and need a strict environment to work more effectively. This practice does not work either. There is no way to force effective performance. To some extent, attendance at work and at the work station can be forced. You can also force people to give the appearance of working. But people do not work well with a whip at their back; they want and need a leader up front, giving them the right tools to work with and showing them the path to follow. Lawrence Appley, former AMA president, used an illustration of trying to move a string across a desk. It is easy to pull it, or lead it, but have you ever tried pushing a string? It's very ineffective.

The only way to significantly increase the effectiveness of paperwork processing, and therefore productivity, is by recognizing and treating the cause of the problem, not the symptoms. The system itself must be improved.

Improving the System

It seems to be commonly accepted today that the way to improve systems is to automate them. The "office of the future" is supposed to solve the problems of high administrative costs, low productivity, unavailable information, and dissatisfied employees. Unfortunately, we've been hearing about the office of the future since the beginning of the business computer age in the mid-1950s. Computerized systems have not yet solved these problems; neither will other machine systems now in use or soon available. In fact, these problems will continue to plague us until we emphasize people-oriented systems rather than machine-oriented ones.

As computers and the other types of machines available to us have come into use, we have seen the development of systems staff groups dedicated to the efficient use of these machines. Methods and procedures departments evolved into computer analysis and programming groups. In many cases, the goal of helping people do their jobs better and easier has been overshadowed by a desire to utilize the full capabilities of the new machine. People have been expected, and sometimes forced, to adapt to new procedures and practices dictated by machine requirements. Many have rebelled, usually passively, against this change.

Many executives recognize this problem. They acknowledge the valuable contribution of the old methods analyst, who knew something about almost everything in the office and could solve procedural problems by working with and helping the people. They also recognize that those days are gone forever. Rapid technological changes have made the systems generalist obsolete in all but the smallest companies. This void in the systems field is being filled by specialists in information handling.

Because most information is still recorded, transmitted, received, or retained on a form of some sort, forms administration is a critical part of the overall information management program in an organization of any size. An effective forms administration program will develop and provide forms and the related processing systems that will help people make the right decisions, or take the right actions, based upon adequate, accurate, but not superfluous information. It will also assure the procurement of those forms at the lowest practical cost to the organization.

As an illustration of the results of an effective forms administration program, here are a few examples from one company:

- Recently, an analyst determined that a special microfilm mailing envelope could be made smaller without affecting its use. The smaller size cut the cost of the form by 25 percent, which amounted to $4,580 per year.
- Another analyst, in reviewing a form ready to be reprinted, suggested and then developed a revised form and procedure that saved one division of the company $75,000 per year. The same system has since been adopted by other groups with additional savings.
- A payroll input form was revised and saved the company about $2,500 per year by allowing more efficient typing and by being provided as a multiple-part set instead of a single sheet that had to be copied or assembled at the time of use.
- A revised purchase contract was developed for a group of continuous computer-output forms at a savings of over $28,000 per year.
- Greater attention to reorder points, reorder quantities, and delivery dates led to a 50 percent reduction in the inventory of compu-

ter forms (saving $273,000) and a 20 percent reduction in the inventory of other forms (saving $135,000).
- Combination buying of all bills of lading centrally, with standardized specifications, saved about 50 percent of the total cost, or about $40,000 per year, according to the supplier.
- Establishing an annual contract with one supplier for all salesbook-type forms saved 20 percent of the prior year's cost. At today's volume, that represents a savings of $25,000 per year.

What could your organization do with a similar effort? The opportunity is there. The results are up to you.

AN EFFECTIVE FORMS ADMINISTRATION PROGRAM

Forms are used by every organization. Our business operations would come to an instantaneous halt if the flow of forms were shut off. Without the information provided by the forms, necessary actions would not be taken, critical decisions would not be made, essential records would not be maintained.

For every form now in use, the following is true:

Someone determined the need
Someone decided what information should be on the form
Someone laid out the lines, captions, and so on
Someone chose the size, construction, paper, and ink
Someone ordered the printing
Someone determined the reorder point and quantity
Someone decided when revisions were needed

In short, the basic activities of a forms administration function occur in every firm. No business, government agency, or any other type of organization can operate without them. However, these activities are usually not effective unless they are part of a forms administration program, which will organize, review, and improve the forms and procedures.

An effective forms administration program consists of three basic parts: control, design, and analysis. We will talk about control, design, and analysis as separate entities and activities. We will study their separate and distinct functions. But we must remember that they are all part of one forms administration program; they are intertwined and interdependent. No forms program can be really effective without all three parts operating together as a unit.

Forms Control

Early efforts to control forms were an outgrowth of paperwork management efforts that began during World War II. The United States government put a lot of work into limiting the enormous amount of paperwork that it generated during those war years.

The first forms control projects in businesses usually evolved from a related function, such as purchasing, office supply, or in-plant printing. Someone in one of these groups would see the need to control the forms being used, and would expand the function of that group to include some centralized forms control activities. Their goals were to reduce the number of forms in use and to reduce the cost of the forms purchased or printed.

Substantial contributions to profit can be made from this concern over the tangible factors affecting the cost of forms. Standard and innovative purchasing techniques, standardized specifications, and adequate but not wasteful quality and quantity determinations were, and are, parts of these forms control activities. They can easily save up to half of the total forms costs.

However, the activities of a forms administration group should not be limited to, or evaluated on, these original objectives. Any function with only these control responsibilities will tend to be ineffective and unaccepted. Their objectives will not be compatible with the users of their service. Forms users want to reduce their paperwork processing efforts. They believe, and rightly so, that better forms will accomplish this—and those better forms might cost more. In addition, there are some cases in which an operation might be better off with more forms, not less. It should be obvious that the control (record-keeping) function is not enough; we also need the analysis of the need and use, and design of the finished product.

Forms Design and Analysis

To understand the importance of these two parts of the forms administration function, we must have a common concept of what a form is. Most people would probably agree that a form is a sheet designed for recording specific data, usually with preprinted headings, captions, lines, boxes, or other devices to guide both the entry and subsequent interpretation and use of that data.

This practical definition is helpful if you have to look at a piece of paper, or other material, and determine whether or not it is a form. But it is not adequate for determining the need for design and analysis. For this, we have to consider a functional definition:

Forms are the medium for transmitting information throughout an organization, the catalysts for getting things done, and the records of what was done. They are the basic tools of our clerical operations.

For example, consider a carpenter's tools. The carpenter could probably get along with one hammer, but no doubt has several in his toolbox. He could have bought them on sale for 69¢ or so at the supermarket or drug store, but he probably paid many times that at a hardware store. Why does he have several expensive tools when a 69¢ one is available? Obviously, hammers designed especially for the different types of nailing to be done will allow the carpenter to produce higher-quality work with less effort. The additional investment in high-quality tools will pay for itself many times over.

Our clerical operations are not conducted with hammers, screwdrivers, or wrenches, but with forms. Just as with a carpenter's tools, the quality of the design of a form has a tremendous impact on its value to the user. Forms design is much more than putting a bunch of lines or boxes on paper, laying out a good-looking form, making the form convenient and easy to print, producing the cheapest form, or combining several forms into one general-use form. All of these are possible results of a good design. But the prime *objective* must be to provide tools that contribute the most value to an organization. This is far different than trying to provide the cheapest and fewest tools. Forms designed with this objective in mind are easier to fill in, are easier to process in all steps of their use, foster a better mental attitude on the part of users (which increases productivity and cuts costs), and, most important, provide consistent and accurate information that enables better decision making.

Well-designed forms do not guarantee increased productivity, they just make it possible. It is not possible to design a form well without analyzing its intended use. To do so would be comparable to building a freeway system without checking traffic patterns first, or to designing a house without first discussing the needs and desires of the buyer. The

9

objective of forms analysis is to determine exactly how each piece of paper flows through the system, how it is used, and, above all, why it is necessary. The analysis prompts recommendations to simplify, combine, or eliminate paperwork processing operations.

In most cases, a form is analyzed in conjunction with the user, and the final responsibility for the system rests with that person or department. The proper forms administration role is to assist the user in any way possible. This is best accomplished by offering ideas and then helping to develop those ideas into viable systems. Throughout the analysis phase, the forms administrator and user must continually ask themselves, "What would I do if this were my business, and I had to pay the bill?"

DISCUSSION

Forms administration is coming of age. The original concept of control, which has caused so much resistance, is giving way to one of cooperation. The rather childish idea of "How can I control and limit the use of forms in order to cut paper costs?" is being replaced by the more mature thought of "How can I help the user do a better job?"

With the correct objectives and attitudes, the understanding of management, and the cooperation of users, forms administration can prove the value of its function.

2

Operating within the Organization

ESTABLISHING THE PROGRAM: A FIVE-STEP PROCESS

If every organization had an effective forms administration program from the first day it opened its doors, poor forms and systems would never develop into sacred traditions. We know from experience, however, that this situation does not exist and probably never will. The practical answer to the question of when to revise existing procedures for buying forms and set up an effective forms administration program is *"Now."* Regardless of the size of the organization, or the procedural environment, the time to move is now. Waiting until next year, next month, next week, or even until tomorrow will cost the stockholders or taxpayers extra dollars because of ineffective paperwork processing. Waiting any longer is an inexcusable management mistake.

Step One: Sell Management

Sell management on the need for greater clerical effectiveness, and on the concept that a forms function will make that improvement possible. I have found the following letter to be persuasive.

TO: DATE:

FROM:

According to national surveys, 30 percent of all working hours in the average corporation are spent processing forms or reports in some manner, and more than one-fourth (28 percent) of that time is wasted because of inefficient forms and procedures.

If our organization is average, we are spending about $_____ (30 percent × payroll costs) each year to process our paperwork, and we are wasting $_____ (8.4 percent × payroll costs) because of inefficient forms and procedures.

We don't know that these figures apply to us. We might be better than average, or we might be worse. In any event, they do indicate the general magnitude of the paperwork problem.

Other organizations have confronted this problem by establishing a forms administration function. Its objectives are to:

- Provide more productive and effective forms.
- Assist other departments in improving their procedures for paperwork processing.
- Ensure the availability of all necessary forms at the lowest practical cost to the organization.

We believe that a similar function could help our company reduce its total paperwork expense, provide better information for decision making, and improve the overall productivity and effectiveness of our administrative operations. We would appreciate a chance to discuss further the establishment of a forms program here.

Thank you for your consideration.

However, this selling process will probably involve more than a single letter or visit, unless the executive involved is already quite aware of the need for paperwork improvement and the part that forms administration can play in it. Samples of current paperwork that illustrate inefficiencies and inadequacies and magazine articles explaining what other organizations are doing can often help make the sale.

In any but the smallest organizations, it should not be necessary to involve top executives. Regardless of the importance of forms administration, senior executives have more important things to consider. Administrative management personnel should be the ones directly involved in approving and establishing the forms function.

In some cases, it helps to have a consultant come in, review the situation, and make recommendations. Many people will accept an outsider's opinions and suggestions more readily than the ideas of their own concerned employees. After the sale has been made, a consultant can help set up a program and get it into operation, if so desired.

Step Two: Select People

Capable people must be selected to staff the forms administration function. Even with management support, the program will not operate effectively without the right people. The job descriptions in Appendix I should be helpful in finding the best people for the jobs.

Step Three: Set Up Procedures

Establish the operating procedures within the forms function and define its relationship to other departments. Emphasize the need for forms administration to see every request for *every* form—new ones, revisions, and reprints.

Step Four: Start Operating

With management support, capable people, and a good system, the next step is to start operating. Begin by routinely ordering all of the forms as they are needed, following an operating system similar to the one described throughout this book (see especially Chapter 8). Build the forms history and the other reference files or records as the forms are ordered.

Step Five: Sell the Service

This is a continuous process. Sell the ability of forms administration to provide a needed service that benefits the users. It takes time, dedicated effort, and proven results to build a reputation and to gain acceptance—there are no overnight miracles.

13

You will note that these five steps do not include the process of collecting multiple samples of all forms as a one-time project at the beginning of the program, nor the crash project of analyzing and classifying each of them in order to quickly build relatively complete files. There may be times when it is advisable to do so between steps three and four; however, it is usually better to get involved immediately in the ordering process. Each form can be more effectively analyzed, classified, redesigned, or possibly eliminated as it is ordered. If a consultant is being used, this collection and classification step could be done at the beginning—to take advantage of the expertise while it is available.

RELATIONSHIP BETWEEN FORMS ADMINISTRATION AND MANAGEMENT

Forms administration reports to the top executives of the organization through various levels of management. A proper relationship with these management levels is critical to the success of any function, including forms administration.

Management Support

Much has been said and written about the need for management support of a forms administration program. Obviously, the implied support of the top executives is needed, just as it is for any other function such as payroll, accounts payable, sales, or inventory control. Written policies and procedures indicate this implied management support. These procedures should include clear, simple instructions for forms users to follow when they need forms.

The active support of the middle manager, to whom the forms administrator reports, is more critical to the success of a forms program. The immediate superior must understand and agree with the program in order to favorably represent it to the next level of management. When starting a program, make sure that everyone concerned understands the objectives. All levels of management should know that the purpose is to improve paperwork processing systems. (The commonly stated objective of reducing the number and cost of forms is a possible result, but it should never be the goal.)

The most important support for a forms program comes from the users. It is absolutely necessary that these customers be satisfied by proven performance. Their satisfaction will ensure the support of administrative management, which in turn will ensure continued support by executive management.

Reporting to Management

The forms function should report on its activities to the next level of management, just as any other department does. What should it report? It is tempting to calculate and report savings. This is a dramatic way to make a point, and it might draw some compliments. The savings that can be documented should be reported. These include lower forms prices due to better purchasing, better specifications, or combination ordering of forms, or smaller inventories due to better control over ordering quantities and reorder points. These savings usually occur when a program is first initiated, and that is when they should be reported. But don't make the mistake of continually calculating and reporting them. That would create the type of unnecessary and wasteful paperwork that the forms group is trying to eliminate. Once it is known and accepted that forms control efforts save money, discontinue the calculations and you'll save more. Obviously, if some unusual savings are made, they should be noted.

Savings in clerical processing costs are real, but usually intangible. There is no doubt that each project worked on will contribute to a more profitable operation. But trying to routinely calculate the amount of those savings is, again, an unnecessary effort and should be done only in unusual circumstances.

How does a forms manager, or a middle manager with responsibility for a forms function, evaluate work efforts and the results of the department? Not by looking for large projects with big dollar savings. There may be a few, but they will not be the norm. The work can be evaluated by the reactions of the forms users, the "customers" of the forms department. Some satisified users will comment on the good performance verbally or in writing. Some will complain about the service they received. Because of the nature of people, a higher percentage of dissatisfied users will complain than satisfied ones will praise. An increasing workload in the forms group is a good indication that the work is done well—it indicates that people are coming back for more help.

Periodic activity reports will help evaluate the workload and the staff level. Activity counts cannot be used as absolute indicators of productivity, but they can indicate general work levels and trends. We have found, for example, that a good analyst can, over a period of time, average about 75 new or revised forms projects per month.

RELATIONSHIP OF FORMS ADMINISTRATION TO OTHER DEPARTMENTS AND USERS

As a staff function providing a service to other parts of the organization, forms administration must have a clear understanding of its relationship to other departments. An effective forms administration group will have direct, personal contact with more people in the organization than any other function. They deal with everyone: beginning file clerks and top executives, elementary school dropouts and Ph.D.'s, newcomers and 35-year veterans.

The people forms administrators come into contact with generally fall into one of the following major groups:

Forms users or requesters
Computer analysts and programmers
Records department personnel
Office supply personnel
In-plant printing or duplicating personnel
Purchasing agents
Suppliers

Relationships among all these groups must be cooperative. In working together, each department or group must do its own unique part to accomplish the most for the organization. Competition for power, authority, or recognition must be avoided.

Depending on the size of the organization, some of these functions may be combined with others, and some may be split up still further. The different functions still exist, however, even if all are performed by one person.

Forms Users

Relationships with the forms users are probably the most important. A real concern must be shown for the problem of each user. Forms personnel handle so many requests for new and revised forms and must deal with so many delivery problems that their jobs can become routine and boring. But, to the person calling on the phone or coming to the office, that problem is a pressing one. An analyst must give each case full attention and become committed to solving the problem.

Analysts must be innovative and creative. Those who go to the forms group for help may not admit it, but they want ideas for improvement. The forms analyst becomes exposed, both inside and outside the organization, to many different ideas. By remembering these ideas, visualizing them to fit needs as they arise, the analyst can really help the users solve their problems.

Unfortunately, however, many users have to be convinced that a forms administrator is a cooperative partner rather than a restrictive adversary. Part of this stems from the term "forms control" and the original objectives of most forms groups. People do not like to be controlled. A manager of one department feels that another department at the same level should not exercise control over his or her operations. Another reason for lack of acceptance of a forms function is lack of knowledge. Unless it is publicized, many people in the organization may not even be aware that a forms administration function exists. They should be informed of its existence, purpose, and activities.

The forms administration group must recognize that they cannot simply assume the leadership role in paperwork improvement. It must be given to them—not by management edict, but by those they serve. The forms group should emphasize the need for paperwork improvement at every opportunity. By pointing out the problems, showing some examples, and offering solutions, they can get others enthused about possible results. They should not try to make everyone an expert forms analyst or designer, but they should try to get others thinking about their needs and their systems. They can use the company paper or magazine, bulletin boards, posters, brochures, handouts, seminars, or any other available medium to get their message across.

After the publicity has brought in the "customers," the analyst or designer must be able to produce the quality product that was advertised. Even the best advertising in the world cannot sell a bad or

17

mediocre product more than once. Forms users have a right to expect the best every time.

Departments usually have responsibility for their own procedures. Forms administrators should offer managers of other departments general ideas on paperwork improvement so that the users can effectively work on their own systems. Forms administration should have responsibility for ordering and reordering all forms for the users. The order quantities and lead times should be based on historical data and the user's estimate of future usage, adjusted by quantity breaks, inventory levels, and so on. Another basic forms administration responsibility is to design the forms, based on the user's needs. The user assists in this area, but the forms group should have final responsibility.

Computer Analysts and Programmers

When a computer systems group does its own forms design, the input and output forms have a tendency to become machine oriented rather than people oriented. This is not a criticism of computer systems departments, but a reflection of our human tendencies. Computer programmers should be given special help in designing the needed forms, and forms administration should have final responsibility for the design, just as they do for non-computerized forms.

Preparing the best form possible requires the utmost cooperation between the computer systems group and the forms group. There is no room for interdepartmental jealousies or conflicts. Each must recognize that it is a part of the overall systems team.

Records Department

Competition can sometimes occur between forms and records groups. The distinction between forms administration activity and records management should be clarified to avoid overlap of responsibility.

Every form used by an organization must be planned, provided, prepared, processed, and preserved. The first two steps, planning and providing, are responsibilities of a forms group. The last step, preserving, is the prime responsibility of the records function. (The other two steps, preparing and processing, are the responsibility of the using department.)

Having the forms and records functions in an organization under the same management will help ensure cooperation, sharing of information, and the development of broader expertise in both groups.

Office Supply

The office supply function, which can go under many names, is the group responsible for the physical handling (receiving, storing, shipping, distribution, and controlling) of forms. Forms administration has to keep the office supply group informed of orders placed, due dates, costs, restrictions, and so on. Likewise, office supply has to notify forms administration when the balance on hand for any item reaches the reorder point, and has to furnish the data on usage that forms administration needs to determine reorder quantities.

The reputation of each function is partially dependent on the performance of the other. Because so many problems can arise after an order has been placed and before the material has been delivered to the user, it is easy for an antagonistic relationship to develop between these two groups. Both must understand that cooperation is necessary to the effective functioning of both groups.

In-House Printing

In an average organization, most forms can be printed by an in-house facility, if one is available for use. With full-service capability, the in-house printshop will probably be the source of more forms than all outside suppliers combined.

It is critical that no numbered forms be printed unless the order originates in forms administration. If this rule is broken, the forms administration program will not be an effective one.

Purchasing

The purchasing function is responsible for buying the forms requested by forms administration from an acceptable supplier. They follow normal purchasing procedures, just as if they were buying any other custom-made product.

Forms personnel must be careful not to usurp purchasing's responsibility for supplier selection, although they may, at times, suggest suppliers. Purchasing must refer to forms administration any request for a form that did not originate in the forms group. This is the only way to be sure that the form is needed, is properly designed, and is not already available.

Suppliers

A good working relationship with representatives of the forms suppliers is very important to the success of a forms administration program. Suppliers can help solve and sometimes prevent problems that arise in creating and delivering a custom-made product. They can also provide valuable assistance in their area of expertise. Consult with them about construction possibilities, paper and carbon recommendations and testing, and other information they have access to as a result of their broad exposure.

Most suppliers can and will provide any forms administration services that an organization is willing to turn over to them. A large company with a forms administration function and a purchasing department probably doesn't need or want anything from the supplier but the basics (delivery of an acceptable product, at an acceptable price, on the date requested). Suppliers should expect to compete for a job with other equally qualified suppliers on a bid basis.

A company with a forms "control" function (an ordering department for forms) and a purchasing department probably uses supplier assistance for forms design. When possible, the supplier should be consulted *before* the order is entered, not after. That requires a good working relationship between the supplier, the forms group, the user, and purchasing. Orders for a supplier-designed form should not be opened to bids.

A company with no forms program or with just the beginning of one will probably turn to the supplier for assistance in the analysis and design of forms, and also for help in inventory management. In this case, the supplier's representative would work directly with the purchasing agent.

3

Forms Control

FORMS control involves monitoring all of the forms used by an organization. This includes:

Ordering forms
Deciding whether or not to stock a form
Selecting the manufacturer (in-house or outside)
Controlling inventory
Allocating costs
Recognizing and disposing of obsolete forms

THE ORDERING PROCESS

Unless the forms administration department is routinely involved with every order for printing every form, it can never be really effective. Each order must orginate in the forms department, so it can be reviewed for:

- Possible or required revisions to the form
- Quantity adjustments, based on usage (past and future) and on price breaks available from printers
- Possibility of combining orders for similar forms
- Complete and accurate specifications

A good order processing system will include the following features, which are discussed in greater detail in Chapter 8.

• A special job ticket/specification form for printing to be done by the in-plant shop. This form will be available only to the forms group, and no orders for forms will be taken by the printshop unless they are written on this form.

• A specification sheet that must be supplied with every requisition for forms to be printed by an outside supplier. This form, again, is available only to the forms group, and the purchasing agent will not process any requests to print forms unless they are accompanied by a specification sheet that has been signed by the forms manager or analyst.

• Notification from the inventory control function that the balance on hand has reached the reorder point previously determined by the forms administration group. The inventory control operation will normally be part of the supply function, but reorder points and quantities should be calculated by forms administration.

• Notification to the user or requester of the form that it is about to be reordered. This gives the user an opportunity to make revisions or to notify forms administration of changes in the usage pattern of the form.

• Routine reordering of the form based on past usage if the user does not reply within a certain period, such as ten working days. This procedure serves two purposes: First, it ensures that a delay in responding to the reprint notice will not result in a back-order situation. Second, it eliminates unnecessary paperwork—the user with no changes to make can simply discard the notice.

• Use of a copier to produce the copies of orders, specifications, and layouts needed in the ordering routine. Transcribing information from one document to another is extremely time consuming. Specifications written in pencil can be photocopied many times. In addition to saving time, this procedure will eliminate costly mistakes that are introduced when information is transcribed by hand. Specification changes can be made very easily, when necessary, by erasing the old information and entering the new. The original pencil-written sheet is always kept on file in the form's folder.

• Direct contacts between forms personnel and supplier representatives. The purchasing department should not try to answer questions about the specifications, design, or construction of the form. Questions from the supplier should be referred to the analyst or coordinator who is familiar with the form. It is the purchasing group's responsibility to select the supplier and to control and monitor the entire purchasing process—not to design the forms. (Of course, these two functions can be combined in some organizations; I know of some cases in which this combination works very well. But it should be remembered that in those situations one person is doing two separate functions.)

• Recording all orders on an order register, and indicating the type of order (whether new, revised, or reprint), where it is to be shipped, and the date due. (When more than one analyst is involved, the analyst's initials should also be shown for reference purposes later and for activity counts.)

• Recording the completion of every order on the order register. This makes it easy to identify and follow up on old, incomplete orders.

• Receipt of samples of every order, from both in-house and outside suppliers. These samples should be reviewed for quality and accuracy and should be filed in the form's folder.

• Use of annual contracts, blanket orders with releases by forms administration, and any other purchasing techniques to reduce as much as possible the amount of routine paperwork in the purchasing process.

STOCK VS. NON-STOCK

Deciding whether or not to stock a form should be the responsibility of the forms administration department. Forms used by several or many departments should be stocked by a central office supply department so they will be immediately available. The expense of maintaining the inventory is more than offset by the savings in printing costs.

Generally, forms used by only one department or at only one location should not be stocked by the office supply group. If enough lead time is allowed for delivery of a reorder, the using group can simply maintain its own stock. As indicated in the discussion on form numbering systems (see Chapter 8), the form number should indicate the non-stock status of that form. The ordering routine for the using department should also be very simple, to encourage proper ordering.

In some cases, forms used by just one department will be stocked.

If the lead time needed to obtain forms purchased from an outside supplier is long, users cannot really be expected to order in sufficient time. (I have yet to find a forms user who can understand a two- to three-month lead time for forms purchases—even seasoned forms administrators have trouble.)

If the quantities purchased are too large for storage in the using department's area, the forms are often stocked by central office supply. However, inadequate space should not be a continuing reason for this inefficient process of maintaining two inventories of the same item.

SELECTING THE MANUFACTURER (IN-HOUSE OR OUTSIDE)

If there is a capable in-plant printshop, many of the forms needed could be supplied by either the in-plant shop or an outside supplier. Because the paperwork required to process an order differs depending on where the order will be filled, the forms administration department should decide what printshop to use before the order is entered.

Usually, if the in-house shop is capable of producing the form, it will be cheaper to have it prepared by that shop. However, requests for large quantities will overload the in-plant shop, and other types of printing will suffer. Also, the shop may not be accustomed to meeting certain quality requirements. Therefore, the capabilities and limitations of the in-plant shop should be reviewed very carefully with the printing manager. Remember, the in-plant shop was not set up just to supply forms, nor was it set up to compete with outside printers or forms manufacturers. If the shop is capable of printing some of the simpler forms, by all means use it; it helps to absorb the shop's overhead. It would probably not be practical to expand the shop in order to print more forms. In most cases, the amount saved by internal printing of forms does not warrant additional investment in space, equipment, or personnel.

One area that should be explored with the in-house shop is the production of carbonless unit sets, using pre-collated paper and the "fan-set" padding compound. (See Chapter 7.) This is a very simple process, requiring no special equipment, and enables the forms group to design forms with the right number of parts even if the quantities are small. The development of this process has been one of the biggest aids to proper forms design and usage in recent years. Multiple-part unit sets, with interleaved carbon, have been available for many years, but the minimum order quantities required by forms manufacturers restricted their use. The pre-collated carbonless set makes it possible to economically produce unit-set forms whenever they are called for.

INVENTORY CONTROL

Most forms groups do not actually handle forms inventory or storage—that is usually done by a supply department. You should, however, be familiar with your organization's inventory control systems so you can be sure they are working properly.

If users cannot obtain a supply of forms when they order it, if they receive the wrong forms, if they receive damaged or shopworn forms, they will be dissatisfied—and rightfully so. And forms administration is usually blamed. Even though forms administrators may not have responsibility for the inventory control function, they should be involved in it. The reputation and acceptance of their function depends on it.

An inventory control system may be fully automated on a computer or it may be a very simple manual system. Regardless of the size or complexity, every system should provide the following information:

Usage, receipts, and balances
Security (theft protection)
Indicators of record-keeping and order-filling accuracy
Clues to trouble spots
Customer satisfaction
Historical and current data on
    Order quantities
    Reorder points
    Safety stocks
    Lead time
    Average usage
    Back-order statistics
    Slow-moving or obsolete items

As an auditor I was concerned with security, accuracy, clues to trouble spots, back-order statistics, and information on slow-moving or obsolete items, which are good indicators of how well the system is operating.

As a computer systems analyst, I was concerned with the methods and techniques of calculating historical and current data. We had to be sure not only that the information was developed correctly from a mathematical standpoint, but that it meant something to those who would use it. To some extent, past information is important only if it can help guide future actions and decisions.

As a branch office manager, and now as a forms manager, I'm concerned with all of these factors, because each one affects customer satisfaction and the total inventory investment. So it's important for me to be involved in decisions about safety stocks, lead times, reorder points, and order quantities.

In organizations that have a manual forms inventory system, the supply department usually maintains the actual inventory records. When the balance on hand of any item reaches the reorder point, the supply group notifies the forms group. At that time, the new reorder quantity and reorder point is calculated using a simple formula, a generous amount of common sense, and the judgment that comes from experience.

In developing the formula, several factors must be considered. First, the reorder point must allow for adequate lead time to get the new shipment in before the supply on hand runs out. That means taking into consideration (1) the time needed to approve a reprint or to develop a revision, (2) the time needed to place an order, and (3) the time needed to manufacture the form.

Another factor in the reorder point calculation is the amount of safety stock needed. Because of variations in usage and possible delays in the ordering or manufacturing process, it is best to plan on having a balance equivalent to one month's supply on hand at the time the new shipment is expected. That means that for forms printed in an internal printshop, a reasonable reorder point is reached when the amount on hand represents a 2½-month supply. For purchased forms, a 3-month figure is satisfactory. It usually takes longer to obtain purchased forms because the ordering procedures are more detailed and the manufacturing requirements more complex.

Order quantities, too, are based on many factors. First, the usage pattern must be determined and considered. If all other factors are equal, the order quantity of a form with consistent usage may be less than that for a form with large month-to-month variances in usage. If two forms are used in the same quantity, but one is used by just one department and the other is used by many, the order quantity for the single-user form can usually be smaller. In general, as more variables are present in the usage pattern, the order quantity will increase. For example, let's look at our own personal financial situation. If all of our bills came due just once a year, at the same time, we would have a great deal of difficulty paying them if we continued to be paid on a weekly, or monthly, basis. We would have to be paid once a year. For most of us, bills are spread throughout the year, and usually throughout the month. This makes it practical for us to be paid in smaller increments. Likewise, forms used consistently throughout the year can be ordered in smaller quantities.

The probability and frequency of revision will also affect the reorder quantity. If future changes are expected, the order quantity should be reduced to minimize the number of forms that will become obsolete when the change is made.

From the cost standpoint, the stock should be kept small to minimize the inventory investment. However, the cost per form usually decreases as the quantity ordered goes up. These two conflicting goals must be balanced to achieve an effective control program.

The reorder point and reorder quantity formula with which I am most familiar uses the guide shown in Table 1.

Table 1. Form reorder quantities based on annual usage.

Purchased Forms	Reorder point: 3-month supply
Annual usage quantity	*Reorder quantity*
Fewer than 5,000 forms	12 months' usage
5,000–10,000 forms	5,000 forms
10,000–50,000 forms	6 months' usage
50,000–100,000 forms	25,000 forms
More than 100,000 forms	3 months' usage
Internally Printed Forms	Reorder point: 2½-month supply
Annual usage quantity	*Reorder quantity*
Fewer than 5,000 sheets *	12 months' usage
5,000–10,000 sheets	5,000 sheets
10,000–60,000 sheets	6 months' usage
60,000–90,000 sheets	30,000 sheets
More than 90,000 sheets	3–4 months' usage

* The sheet quantities have to be converted from the number of forms when multiple-part forms are involved.

Following these guidelines has resulted in an average inventory level of about a 6-month supply, a back-order (out-of-stock) rate of 1 percent of the total item lines ordered on an inventory of 3,000 forms, and an order volume of about 7,000 lines per month. About 275 of these items are reordered each month.

In the case of computer output forms, usage is usually more easily predicted. However, the possibility of computer reruns must be considered. Also, there is a difference between stock tab (essentially blank paper) and custom forms (those with a printed format on the paper). On the stock tab forms, the necessity for safety stock and other lead-time factors is very minimal. On these normally high-volume items, an annual order with weekly or monthly releases is quite practical. The on-hand inventory of these would seldom be more than a 2- to 5-week supply.

On custom-printed continuous forms, the opposite is true. The need for a safety stock is greater. There is usually no alternate form available for emergency use. The information system is locked in to that specific output document. An out-of-stock situation simply cannot be tolerated. Production time of these continuous forms is also longer than for other types of form constructions. As a result, a reorder point of a 5- to 6-month usage is normally required. In most cases, a 12-month supply would be ordered, with several releases if the quantity exceeds about 400,000 plies.

These guidelines for ordering continuous forms have resulted in a 2- to 2½-month supply on hand, and no unplanned out-of-stock situations. This is for an inventory of about 300 items, and about 30 reorders per month.

We have been looking at inventory control over items stocked by a supply department. There are other situations to consider also.

Some forms can be shipped directly to the using group by the manufacturer or the internal printshop. The user is then responsible for inventory control. Conversations with forms people from many companies confirm that forms users cannot be relied upon to order promptly or properly. (Reordering is such a minor and seemingly insignificant part of their job that it tends to be ignored until too late.) If the forms are critical for continued operation, ask users to report the balance on hand at the end of each month. Using this data, the forms group can reorder at the right time. In many cases, orders can be placed for several forms for different locations at the same time, which results in a lower cost per form than if single orders were placed by the user or the forms group. A more consistent design, format, and content is also assured this way.

Many forms suppliers are now offering an inventory management service to their customers. Usually they will take over as much or as little of the entire process as the customer is willing to relinquish. For companies without an established supply operation—and even those with established systems—this can be a very practical and effective alternative. Of course, more forms will be purchased from the supplier providing the service. Some purchasing agents will cringe at the thought of not being able to put most orders out on bids, but the situation is not necessarily bad. A good sales representative can contribute a great deal to effective forms and paperwork systems, but that person needs the assurance of continued business to justify special service.

The supplier's inventory service is not necessarily a replacement of an internal distribution system. It might be used for a certain type of form, or for certain types of users (branch locations, for example), or as a supplement to the existing system for large-volume forms. For example, to save inventory space but still obtain favorable prices, a year's supply of a form might be ordered and printed. The supplier could store the entire quantity, with periodic releases to the customer's supply inventory.

COST ALLOCATION

Almost every time two or more forms managers get together, the subject of cost allocation comes up. Some managers feel that the costs of forms should be charged to one central account no matter who uses them and regardless of whether they are inventoried or sent directly to the users. These managers recommend that an annual budget be set up for the cost of forms and that the forms group be responsible for keeping the costs within budget.

Others maintain that the using department should pay directly for any forms purchased especially for them by an outside supplier or printed just for them by the internal printshop. On the other hand, if the forms were used by more than one department, and were stocked by a supply group, there would be no recharge to the using departments.

Still others would charge the users for all purchased forms and not charge them for any internally produced forms.

The rest of the group argues that all forms should be charged to the department that uses them, regardless of where they are printed, supplied, or stocked.

Although these discussions are very interesting, they are usually quite futile—the forms group is limited by whatever accounting system has been established in the organization. For example, if the printshop does not have a cost system to determine the cost of producing each job, there is no way that the cost of forms produced in that printshop can be recharged to the users. Unfortunately, this is the case in many organizations.

Likewise, if the inventory of office supplies and forms is not maintained as an inventory account in the financial records, there is no adequate way of recharging the cost of forms withdrawn from that inventory to the various departments. This, too, is a common problem.

As an accountant, auditor, and office manager, it seems to me that there is only one right way to allocate the cost of forms. Charge all forms to the using departments at the time they receive them from the printer or from stock. Other techniques may be more expedient or cheaper, but in this aspect of our forms management program we should be looking for the method that contributes the most to the operation.

A department manager should be held responsible for the total cost of operating that department. Obviously, costs include salaries, equipment, building overhead, an allocated share of utilities and other costs that might be beyond the control of the individual managers, and the cost of all supplies—including forms—that are used by that department. The absence of accountability for costs can lead to a lack of concern about expenses. Managers who are not responsible for the cost of forms are less likely to worry that a "rush" job is expensive, or that a multicolor print job often adds unnecessary costs. Managers who are held accountable for those costs will show greater sensitivity to them.

Cost Allocation System

The system used to allocate the cost of forms can range from the very simple to the very complex depending upon the organization. Of course, any system must be compatible with the accounting system used by the organization.

Most organizations indicate on the purchase order where the cost of the purchased item is to be charged. If the form is used by only one department and is delivered directly to that department rather than to a supply group, the using department should be charged at the time of purchase. If, however, the material is purchased and put into an inventory to be withdrawn by various departments or by just one department, the costs should be charged to an inventory account, and then charged to the using departments when the forms are withdrawn from stock. This requires the use of an order form or requisition to withdraw materials from stock, which becomes the source document for the acounting transaction. In some organizations, the allocation is based on a handwritten list of quantities, costs, and departments. This list is summarized monthly and charged to the various accounts. In other organizations, the data is fed into a computer for recharging and for inventory management.

If your in-house printshop does not have a cost allocation system, perhaps you should help it establish one. Most large printshops charge the cost of the time and material for each individual job to the requester of that job. This is the ideal way of handling the printing costs, especially those for printing forms.

If a job cost accounting system is not or cannot be established, then perhaps a standard or average price list could be developed for the type and quantity of forms normally produced by that printshop. This list could be much like price lists used by the "instant" printers around the country. The total amount charged out to requesters on the standard cost system could then be compared with the total costs of operating the department, and some measure of efficiency developed.

So far, the discussion of cost allocation has considered only the costs of physically producing the form: the costs of composition, plate-making, press time, paper, and so on. I do not believe that the costs of analyzing the system or designing the form should be directly charged to the requester. This would tend to discourage use of the service by many functions within the organization. There would be a tendency for a department manager to first think in terms of how much an analyst would cost rather than the service that could be provided.

Most people could develop their own forms (and may have been doing so for many years), so there would be a strong tendency to avoid the forms management group if analysis and design time were to be recharged. This situation would not benefit anyone in the organization.

THE RECOGNITION AND DISPOSITION
OF OBSOLETE FORMS

An effective forms administration function must be routinely concerned over the recognition and disposition of obsolete, unusable forms. Forms become obsolete as user needs and government requirements change.

Some forms become obsolete when the content or construction needs to be modified. In most cases, proper planning by the user and designer will minimize the number of forms that must be discarded. Every time a form is revised, the forms analyst must decide, based on the needs of the users of the form, whether to use or destroy the existing version. If the old version is to be used up before the new one is distributed, the normal first-in, first-out inventory rotation will accomplish this. Here is where the revision letter suffix or the revision date becomes very important on the form, the packaging, and on the inventory records (see the section on numbering systems in Chapter 7). If immediate use of the new revision is required, the old version should be destroyed at once to eliminate confusion. The cost of the destroyed forms should be charged to the department requiring the change. This tends to reduce the number of times alterations of this sort occur.

The type of obsolescence that occurs when a form is revised is easy to recognize. But if the form or the information is no longer used and the entire system has been scrapped, the forms group may be the last to know.

In theory, users notify forms administration when this happens; but in practice, this doesn't usually happen.

If the office supply department notifies forms administration that a form has not been withdrawn from stock for an agreed upon period of time (one year works well), forms administration can then check with the users to see if the form is really obsolete. It is possible that the user over-ordered, or that usage dropped considerably since the last order. It is not safe to automatically assume a form is obsolete just because it has not been ordered from stock for a year, or any other reasonable period. If the user confirms that the form is no longer used, it should be withdrawn from inventory and destroyed. The cost should be charged to the user.

In the case of forms that are not stocked, there is no central inventory to be destroyed when a form becomes obsolete. The user simply stops ordering the form. However, the printshop must be notified so the plate file can be destroyed, and forms administration needs to update the files to show the current obsolete status.

An easy way to monitor this type of obsolescence is to put a colored tab on each file folder the first time it is ordered each year. During the second year, a different color tab is put on the folder; the next year, another color, and so on. It is then easy for the forms coordinators to review the files and pull out all forms that have not been ordered for a set period of time, such as two years.

The users are then asked about the status of these forms. Once again, it is not unusual for a form that has not been ordered for two years to still be active. If the form is no longer used or will not be ordered again, forms administration can mark its records accordingly, and notify the in-plant shop to destroy the negatives and plates on their shelf.

4

Forms Analysis

Forms analysis is the process of finding out how the form is going to be used, or how it is being used in the case of one about to be revised. It is, in most cases, a cooperative effort between the user and the analyst. Analysis might take a few minutes on one form and many hours on another. It is important that those designing the form be familiar with the department that will be using it.

Some designers like to follow an established pattern of analysis; most use a checklist of some sort as an aid. In many instances, a flowchart is useful. Regardless of the technique used, the attitudes of both the analyst and the user are very important to the ultimate success of the effort. Each one must be concerned about providing the best possible tool, and be willing to work with other people to achieve that goal.

Forms analysis efforts are basically problem-solving efforts. I like to define forms analysis as "the creative, innovative application of knowledge and abilities to the basic problem of the user in order to provide the best possible tool."

Like any other problem-solving situation, there are some basic steps involved in paperwork analysis. These are outlined in this chapter.

IDENTIFY THE PROBLEM

The first step in analysis is to find out what the problem is. If a paperwork processing system is already in existence, look for potential

35

problems in that system, barriers to productivity in the present forms, and evidence of inadequate or inaccurate information.

For a new form, it means determining the real objective, the real need—and this can be very different from the expressed need when the request is made for the new form. Generally, *major* problems will be apparent to the people using the system. As an example, a bottleneck in paper flow that prevents people from finishing their work on time will be recognized. A poorly designed form that promotes errors or provides bad information could also be easily recognized.

However, most problems in paperwork handling are relatively minor. People will use an ineffective form for many years without knowing they are wasting a lot of time and effort to record and maintain unnecessary or misleading information. The items that follow should be discussed with users, to acquaint them with the many minor problems that can afflict a form or processing system. Correction of those numerous minor problems will make a significant improvement in the overall system.

Paperwork Preparation

Using unofficial forms is a common practice. People who need some information type their questions on a sheet, leaving room for answers, and then make copies of that "form" for use. In most cases, these forms are difficult to use. The questions are hard to understand, the answer space is either too large or too small, multiple parts are needed but are not provided, and identification of the organization and form is either inadequate or missing.

Those who originate these forms think they are saving money for their organization. In fact, a typed form that has been copied or duplicated is probably the most expensive one. Even more important, the information gathered in this manner is likely to be inadequate and inaccurate for proper decision making.

Filling out a form by hand and then typing it is another common wasteful practice. There is no reason to type most forms—it's usually a duplication of effort and an inexcusable waste of time. Some people feel that *all* business communications, forms or otherwise, should be typed. The only benefits from this practice accrue to the typewriter supplier. Our need is for effective and efficient gathering of the information, not for formal documents.

One very common lame excuse for this time-waster is, "No one can read my writing!" In other words, this individual (usually a male management-level employee) is saying that the organization should pay for unnecessary secretarial work because of his admitted failure to learn one of the most basic skills taught to everyone from the first grade on up. Even if the person's writing is bad, most forms should be printed anyway, and practically everyone can print legibly.

Another reason for this practice is very subtle, but still real: Many people attach importance to the boss–secretary relationship as a status symbol. Procedures in which the boss provides handwritten forms to the secretary for typing help to assure that this status will not be changed.

Transcribing data from one sheet to another should be scrutinized. In some cases, adding another part to the original form will eliminate the need for copying the information. (This might require some revision of the original to make it serve two purposes.) If the transcription is necessary, the information should be in the same sequence on the two documents. The greatest problem with transcribing data is the possibility of introducing errors while transcribing, especially when working with numbers.

Writing memos on all or most phone conversations, and requiring written confirmation of verbal conversations are measures taken primarily to protect or defend one's actions. As this does not serve any productive purpose, the practice should be eliminated as much as possible. Memos and confirmations that will help guide future actions and decisions are important, and well-designed forms should be available for that purpose. But there is no need for a defensive paperwork system in a well-run organization.

Preparing manual tallies or records to check computer data is still done in some companies. It's a carry-over from the old days of card punch, sort, list, tabulate, and so on. In general, this is a waste of time with today's computer systems.

Requiring approvals on routine items wastes time and paper. If two or more management levels have to approve a transaction, that implies that the judgment of every level below the top one is not trusted for that transaction. (This occurs most visibly in the supermarket when the check-out clerks must call the manager to approve each check. The check-out lines are held up while the manager routinely initials each check—usually without asking any questions and without recognizing the customer.)

Making multiple-part forms using single sheets and carbons is another practice that is inefficient, costly, and time consuming. This is easily corrected by an adequate system for providing the necessary paperwork tools.

Typing a number of similar letters or reports can usually be reduced by preprinted forms, notices, form letters, or a word-processing system with stored letters, paragraphs, or phrases. With all of these methods available to originate information once for repeated use, no one should have to retype the same information many times.

Paperwork Processing

Making copies of a form for distribution or filing is another indication of inadequate tools. It is much more efficient to include the necessary parts in the form when it is manufactured.

Sending forms, reports, or letters to people who don't need them is inexcusable. If an individual is not expected to make any decision or take any action as a result of the document, don't send it.

Involving several people when one is enough, handling single transactions rather than batches of them, and following disorganized work patterns are all indications that the work flow patterns should be revised to be more productive, smoother, and simpler.

Using envelopes for nonconfidential interoffice mail can be greatly reduced by using properly designed forms that have addresses preprinted for easy fold-and-mail operations.

Paperwork Filing and General

The problems in this category are not necessarily the result of poor forms design, but they should be reviewed anyway as part of your analysis of the entire paperwork system. These include:

Paperwork filing
- Difficulty in finding information as needed
- Repeatedly expanding file system capacity
- Maintaining duplicate files of the same information
- Filling folders, drawers, and shelves too full for easy access

General
- Making a lot of errors
- Repeatedly needing special reports or studies to make decisions
- Continually handling crisis situations
- Experiencing bottlenecks in work flow

BREAK IT DOWN

After determining the real problem or the real objective of the design, the next step is to find out the details of how the system operates. You can't improve a system if you don't know how it works. Most analysts will not have enough time to get *all* the details about a system, but that's usually not necessary. You need only enough data to understand how the particular form fits in with the rest of the forms and with the system.

To analyze an operation, you have to know:

What is being done
Where it is done
When it is done
Who is doing it
How much is done
How long it takes
How it is done

As you find out how things are done now, question that method and try to think of better ways to do it. This process requires imagination, innovation, creativity, empathy, diplomacy, and common sense.

Flowcharts can be used to graphically illustrate a procedure; they can help analyze the paper flow, help you see alternatives, and help you sell new ideas. These charts can show the work of a person, a group, or several groups. They can show the movement of people or paper over a wider area. Three types of charts are used: layout charts, paperwork flowcharts, and flow process charts.

If you watch football games on TV, you've seen something that resembles these different kinds of flowcharts: the different kinds of camera shots used to inform viewers of what is going on in the game.

The program usually starts with a wide-angle shot of the field and the stands. It gives a good overall view of the situation. You can look at the flags to see if there is any wind; a look at the crowd will tell you about the weather; if it's raining, you can see potential problem areas on the field. This shot is also used for kickoffs and punts, to give you a good feeling for the movement from one end of the field to the other.

When the teams line up for a play from scrimmage, the camera operator zooms in a little to show the players, with the ball in the center of the picture. When the ball is snapped, the camera operator's job is to follow the movement of the ball, keeping it in the center of the screen. This is the shot that keeps viewers most informed about the action of the game. They should be able to see who is handling it and what is happening to it all of the time.

The isolated shot is another one that is very interesting to the viewers, and it's invaluable to a coach trying to improve the performance of his players. This shot is a close-up that shows the movement of one individual. The camera follows that player during an entire play, showing every step, every move taken—including the expression on his face and sometimes even the movement of his eyes. A slow-motion playback shows a player where one step could have been saved or what he did to give away his next move.

This may seem like very minute detail work, and it is. In team sports, good results are possible only when each individual performs in harmony with the rest of the group. Similarly, the paperwork system of an organization is dependent on cooperative, coordinated efforts by all those working in that system. Flowcharts can be used like the camera shots of football games to help improve the performances of each individual.

The layout chart, or flow diagram, is comparable to the wide-angle shot of the football field. It shows movement among people, desks, buildings, and companies. When you take a road map and draw a planned route for a trip on it, you're using a layout chart. This kind of chart can be helpful in showing problems in the physical layout of offices or in pointing out the number of different people involved in a transaction. Just like its counterpart in the football game, it can seldom be used alone.

The paperwork or form flowchart is like the camera that follows the ball. It shows the movement of each piece of paper, and is used to help assess the number of parts needed, the interrelationships among forms, and the possibility of duplication of effort. It is probably the most useful chart for developing and improving forms systems.

The flow process chart is helpful for analyzing the details of how a form is filled out or otherwise processed. Like the camera's isolated shot, it usually shows the actions of one worker. Basically, it's a list of every step taken by an individual to complete a certain activity. There are some standard formats used for this type of chart, but I prefer to simply list the steps in the order they occur. Codes and symbols are usually superfluous for most forms analysis needs.

INFORMATION FLOW ANALYSIS

Use the Information Flow Worksheet at the end of this chapter as a guide for the critical process of finding out how a form will be used. At times, it may be appropriate for the user to fill out the worksheet for a form or a group of forms used in an area. However, it is probably not necessary or advisable to always use this form when discussing a new form or a revision with a user. But the analyst should use it as a tool to review the system before preparing a layout.

Need, Objectives, and Results of This Information

The answers to the first four questions on the worksheet should substantiate the need for the information and the form. However, they are not asked in an attempt to eliminate the form—they are asked so the analyst or designer will fully understand the form's objectives and desired results. If users feel that you are questioning their decision that the information is necessary, they may easily become resentful. Therefore, it is important to convey an attitude of cooperation and assistance rather than one of controlling or limiting the user's information.

Preparation and Processing

After you understand what the user needs, get the details of how the form will be prepared and processed. The answers to the questions in this section of the worksheet provide the information needed to develop a good format and construction using the data elements provided by the user. They can also help you suggest additional information or delete information in order to improve the tool.

How will the form be originated (filled in)? The type of individual

41

originating the form determines the spacing requirements for the form. For example, my experience has shown that production, warehouse, and sales personnel usually write larger than laboratory and clerical employees. The method of preparation is also extremely important in deciding how much space to allow.

The number of users is one factor that influences the kind of instructions that should be included on the form. In general, as more users are involved, more instructions are advisable. This information will also affect ordering quantities, reorder points, and inventory practices.

How many will be used? This information is absolutely necessary to determine how many forms to order, and is also helpful in assessing the potential value of extensive analysis and design efforts. (It is always surprising to find that users are usually thinking of how many forms to order, without knowing how many will be used.)

Is the information on this form used as input to another form or report? Is another form/report used as a source for the information on this form? This information is needed to arrange the data elements on the form in the best sequence for effective transcribing. It can also lead to combinations of forms within the transaction or series of transactions.

Is the form used as a source document for computer input? If so, knowing the method of input will allow the analyst to design an effective input document without affecting the other important uses of the form.

Is there a need for numbering the form? This question is asked so serial numbering will not be used unless absolutely necessary. Also, knowledge of the reason for numbering will help determine whether or not strict inventory controls have to be used to maintain accountability for all numbers.

Are there any usage characteristics that require a specific size, paper, construction, ink, color, and so on? If any unusual or specific features are requested (even asking for an 8½″ × 11″ sheet is a request for a specific size), the analyst must know why so that requirement will not be accidentally dropped in order to standardize or economize.

Could multiple-choice answers help the users provide or understand the information easier or better? All captions on the form and their expected answers must be thoroughly reviewed to answer this question. Many analysts do not take the time to find out what the answers to a form's questions should be. As a result, captions and the answer space can be misleading and they can miss the chance of helping the user do a better job of furnishing or collecting information.

Is there a need for differences in the printing on various parts of the form? Good forms design can often limit the need for part-to-part differences. However, if such differences are clearly necessary they must be considered when planning the layout and the construction. In almost all cases, the form will have to be purchased from a forms manufacturer.

Is there a need for selective imaging on any parts? This used to mean using "Chinese blockouts" or patterned or strip carbons. With the latest methods for sensitizing selected areas on carbonless papers, selective imaging is becoming easier, more economical, and more practical. However, it should be done only when it enhances the usage value of the form.

Distribution, Filing, and Retention

Is the form separated and distributed at one time, or are some parts removed before others? The distribution sequence helps point out construction specifications that will aid rather than hinder the user. As an example, if the third part of a five-part set is to be removed first, it should probably be about ¼″ longer than the other plies so that it can be easily located and removed.

Distribution system; Distribution pattern. Knowledge of this part of the paperwork flow is needed so that the finished form can be distributed smoothly, economically, and effectively. As an example, a form sent individually through the postal system should be designed for use with a window envelope. If other parts of the same form are sent through an interoffice mail service in a batch, they should be designed for a standard multiple-use interoffice envelope.

Filing system. The layout and construction should accommodate the filing system and equipment that will be used. In some cases, even the direction of the grain of the paper makes a significant difference.

The retention period must be known in order to select the proper paper. Newsprint cannot be used for permanent records, and 100 percent rag paper is inappropriate for a telephone message memo.

Microfilming. Filming should be done from the original whenever possible. However, other parts can be used if the legibility, image contrast, and paper color are satisfactory. Some testing may be required to assure acceptable films.

43

BUSINESS FORMS MANAGEMENT

INFORMATION FLOW WORKSHEET

Need, Objective, and Results of this Information	
What actions or decisions are dependent on the information developed or distributed?	
How is this action or decision initiated now, without this requested information?	
What would happen if this information were not available?	
How will this new or changed information improve the productivity or effectiveness of our information system?	

Preparation and Processing

How will the form be originated?	Type of Individual			No. of users
	☐ Prod./Whse ☐ Laboratory ☐ Sales ☐ Clerical ☐ Supervisory ☐ Other:			

Preparation Method

Manual	Man. T/W	Elec. T/W-Reg.	Elec. T/W-Ball	Computer (specify Printer Model)
☐ Pen	☐ 10/inch Pica	☐ 10/inch Pica	☐ 10/inch	☐
☐ Pencil	☐ 12/inch Elite	☐ 12/inch Elite	☐ 12/inch	☐ Other (specify)

How many will be used?	Quantity	Unit (Ea., Bk., etc.)	Period	Comments

Is another form/report used as a source for the information on this form?	☐ No ☐ Yes Explain	Attach Completed Sample
Is the information on this form used as input to another form or report?	☐ No ☐ Yes Explain	Attach Completed Sample
Is this form used as a source document for computer input?	☐ No ☐ Yes Explain (input method and which part)	
Is there a need for numbering the form?	☐ No ☐ Yes Explain	
Are there any usage characteristics that require a specific size, paper, construction ink, color, etc.?	☐ No ☐ Yes Explain	
Could multiple-choice answers help users provide or understand the information easier or better?	☐ No ☐ Yes Explain	
Is there a need for differences in the printing between parts?	☐ No ☐ Yes Explain	
Is there a need for selective imaging on any parts?	☐ No ☐ Yes Explain	

Distribution, Filing, and Retention							**420**
Is the form separated and distributed at one time, or are some parts removed before others?		☐ One-time distribution ☐ Other (explain)					
		Part 1	Part 2	Part 3	Part 4	Part 5	Part 6
DISTRIBUTION SYSTEM	Postal System						
	Interoffice Mail						
	Delivery						
	Other (specify)						
DISTRIBUTION PATTERN	Individually						
	Batches of this form (qty. or frequency)						
	Combined with other "mail"						
FILING SYSTEM	Filing sequence						
	Filing equipment						
	Retention period						
Indicate any parts that are eventually microfilmed (Show when they are filmed.)							

Comments — Further Explanations

5

Forms Design and Evaluation

In the process of forms design, all the information provided by the user and determined through analysis is taken into account to develop the best possible tool. This process can be compared to an architect taking the information gathered from a home-buyer and designing a custom home that fits the needs of that specific family, while still using standard components and techniques to maintain the lowest practical cost to the buyer.

Forms design does not include composition, which is the preparation of camera-ready copy. This is part of the printing process. (The architect's job does not include actually building the home he's designed.) Designers are usually too busy with the duties of their position to be responsible for the more mechanical, yet vitally important, composition work. However, if time is available the two jobs may be combined. This is fine as long as all concerned recognize that two different jobs are being performed.

Well-designed forms are easier to fill in and easier to use throughout all steps of their processing. They provide better and more accurate information, which enables better decision making, and they create a better mental attitude in those using them, which can increase productivity and cut costs.

No form can be designed properly unless it has been thoroughly analyzed. The designer must know how information will be entered on the form, and therefore needs to find out:

- Whether or not it is typed, and, if it is, which typewriter will be used
- What other preparation or processing equipment will be used
- If it is handwritten, and by whom
- Under what conditions the form will be prepared; whether at a desk, on a clipboard, while hand-held, or even while driving a forklift truck down a dark, narrow aisle of a warehouse
- The quantity of forms filled out by an individual and in total
- Who will read the form
- The physical environment when read
- The quantity of forms read at one time or by one individual
- Whether there are any special considerations, for example: "Primarily filled out or read by older people with failing eyes," and so on

This sounds like a lot of detail, and it is. Unrelenting attention to detail is absolutely essential in order to properly design a good form.

THE TEN COMMANDMENTS OF FORMS LAYOUT

I don't claim to be a prophet (I don't even have a beard) and these commandments are not divinely inspired or written in stone, but I would like to outline the basic techniques or standards of forms layout using the ten commandments of forms layout. If all forms users and designers would follow these guidelines, we'd have much better forms to work with and much greater paperwork efficiency.

1. Use 3-by-5 spacing
2. Use ULC design
3. Select captions that clearly define the information desired
4. Place check boxes in front of the answers
5. Use screens and other visual aids to help guide the eyes, not for decoration
6. Provide adequate margins
7. Make the form self-instructing
8. Show the distribution and routing of parts on the form

9. Show a form number and meaningful title on every form
10. All lines and words on the form should guide the entry, interpretation, and use of information.

These standards of forms layout should become part of the forms analyst's daily work habits. They should be applied almost automatically in response to any given design situation. Analysts will depart from the standards in unusual situations in order to accomplish the overall objective of providing the best tool. But when they make an exception, it is done deliberately.

Now let's look at each one of these in detail to see why they are important considerations when designing a useful, valuable tool for administrative employees.

1. 3-by-5 Spacing

Allowing the right amount of space on a form is one of the most important things to consider when thinking about the usefulness of a form. Too much or too little space will cause people to wonder if they are giving the appropriate answer. It may look as if the originator expected either a longer or a shorter answer than what is apparently correct.

Most forms are either typed or handwritten, usually depending on the user's preference. Therefore, a well-designed form will be spaced so that it can be efficiently prepared either way. To allow for this dual method of preparation, the 3-by-5 system (three writing lines per inch vertically, five characters per inch horizontally) is very effective.

Vertical Spacing
Three writing lines per inch will accommodate the handwriting of most people:

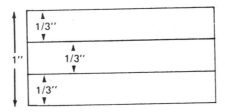

In general, people who fill in forms regularly write quite small; those not accustomed to writing a great deal usually write large. Proper forms design will recognize and plan for the wide diversity of writing styles among forms users.

Three lines per inch is also ideal for typewritten responses, as it matches the double spacing on the typewriter. Forms should always be designed so that the typist can use the double-space return lever. It should never be necessary to move the platen an uneven number of lines. However, some models of IBM typewriters have a nonstandard 5.28-line-per-inch spacing as an aid to typing correspondence. These typewriters cannot be used effectively for filling in many forms.

Horizontal Spacing

For answers of up to ten characters, allow 1″ for every five characters in the entry as shown.

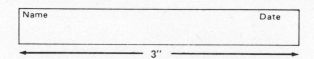

For answers over ten characters long, allow 2″ plus an inch for every seven to eight characters. This provides adequate space for most types of handwriting and is also good for typed entries.

Most entries will not require all the space provided; this leaves a very desirable "white space" at both ends that helps separate the answer from adjacent data. A full line of words or numbers, separated only by the vertical lines on the form, is very hard to read. Readers can easily misinterpret the information or get discouraged trying to read it—some may even discard the report without using it.

Names of companies or individuals, which will vary a great deal in length, usually fit well in a 3″ horizontal space. When the form calls for a signature and a date, both should fit in that space.

Name	Date

←————————— 3″ —————————→

2. ULC Design

There are many ways of arranging captions and corresponding answer space on a form. Most of them are very inefficient and ineffective. The great majority of people lay out a form like this:

50

EMPLOYEE NAME _____ EMPL. NO. _____

STREET ADDRESS_____ TELEPHONE NO. _____

CITY_____ STATE_____ ZIP CODE _____

Anyone trying to fill out a form like this would have trouble fitting his or her name and other data in the space provided.

A well-designed form uses the ULC (upper left caption) style, in which the same information is presented like this:

Employee Name	Empl. No.
Street Address	
City, State, Zip	Telephone (incl. Area)

The ULC design style (also called box design) is better because:

- The captions become secondary after the fill-in data is entered
- No writing space is used up by the captions
- Typewriter tab stops are easier to set up
- Captions are not hidden by the typewriter mechanism during preparation
- It is easier to provide the proper amount of fill-in space
- The same information can be accommodated on a smaller form or more information on a form the same size

Use of the ULC style practically eliminates the possibility of using a normal office typewriter to prepare camera-ready copy for printing the form. Professional composition equipment, such as a Varitype or an IBM Composer, should be used. It is possible to use a typewriter if the layout is prepared at twice the size of the finished form and then photographically reduced. For example, an 8½" × 11" form would require a 17" × 22" layout. This will reduce the normal typewriter type down to the size used on forms.

Of course, there are times when a number of lines of data are recorded in columns. It is unnecessary, and usually unwise, to repeat the captions on each line. In this case, use column headings: a line of captions across the top of the columnar area.

The height of the caption line depends upon several factors. If all captions will fit on a single line, a ¹⁄₆″ or ¼″ high space is probably adequate. If two lines of type are needed, use a normal ¹⁄₃″ space. Column headings are normally centered horizontally and vertically in the box. Use the same size type as for an upper left caption.

If a series of headings is too long for the column width, the headings can be slanted upward at about a 45- to 60-degree angle or turned sideways and printed vertically.

3. Selecting Captions

In the March 1977 issue of *Graphic Arts Monthly*, J. Kish's article mentioned that applicants for both clerical and professional positions consistently completed their employment applications incorrectly. They had difficulty trying to figure out what the company was asking.

It is very important that captions and other words on every form be understandable by everyone who will be using the form. It is also important that the captions ask the right questions. A caption on a form is a question. The one or two words selected must leave no doubt as to the answer desired. For example, how would you answer this question, a very common one on forms?

Would you enter date *needed*, date *ordered*, date *shipped*, date *requested*, date *approved*, date *hired*, or date *terminated*?

Good captions are not written so that they can be understood by someone familiar with the system; they are written so that someone unfamiliar with the form will not misunderstand them. The advantages of good captions are these:

> They provide better answers, in less time
> They reduce the training time needed for employees
> They reduce or eliminate the need for detailed procedural instructions
> They provide better management information with less effort

As a further reminder of the importance of gathering adequate information before starting to design the form, good captions cannot be selected unless the analyst has determined what the answers are supposed to be.

4. Check Boxes

Place check boxes in front of the answers. This is really a two-part commandment. First it presupposes that you are providing possible answers, then it instructs on the arrangement of those answers and the respondents' indication of the selected answer.

Remember the tests we used to take in school? Most of us preferred true-false or multiple-choice tests to subjective or essay exams. If possible answers were given to us, it was a lot easier to select the best one than it was to come up with the complete answer without any help.

Although subjective exams are probably the best test of a student's knowledge, they also take longer to answer and grade. In business operations, we're usually not trying to test knowledge; we're trying to gather and transmit information as rapidly and accurately as possible. For this reason, possible answers should be provided in a multiple-choice or yes-no format whenever doing so will improve the accuracy or efficiency of filling out or reading the form.

Once you have determined that the answers should be supplied, you'll have to decide how to arrange them. The following illustration shows several ways to arrange the answers to a marital status question on a withholding certificate.

Don't do this:	Marital status —	Single ☐ Married ☐ Single, Head of Household ☐ Married, but spouse filing separately ☐
or this:	Marital status —	Single ☐ Married ☐ Single, Head of Household ☐ Married, but spouse filing separately ☐
Do this: (handwritten)	Marital status:	☐ Single ☐ Single, head of household ☐ Married, filing jointly ☐ Married, but spouse filing separately

or this:
(typed)

Marital Status

☐ Single	☐ Single, head of household	☐ Married, filing jointly	☐ Married, but Spouse filing separately

An exception to the rule of placing the check boxes in front of the answers is the case of a series of questions with yes-no answers. Here, the reader must read the entire question, decide on the answer, and check the appropriate box. The most logical place to put the yes-no answer is at the right—where the reader's eyes are when he's finished reading the question. The answers can be arranged either in two vertical rows of boxes or in two columns with yes-no headings.

Proper application of this principle also requires that the designer know what the answers should or could be. Thorough analysis of each question and expected answers is important. No form can be properly designed without this analysis.

Understanding the reasons for providing possible answers will sometimes lead to a decision to omit those answers. If the person filling out the form is likely to know the answer and could quickly fill it in, it might be easier to write out the answer than to find and check the right box. For example, in most cases there is no advantage to preprinting "Male" and "Female" as answers to "Sex." The caption itself is clear and definite, and everyone knows the possible answers and their own answer. The same is true for "Marital Status" on most forms. However, in the example just shown, the answers are terms or phrases not normally used except on a tax return. In that case, a blank fill-in space would not yield the desired information.

When giving instructions on forms with check boxes, ask that an X be drawn rather than a ✔. Regardless of how carelessly the X is made, the intersection of the two lines will almost always be in the appropriate box. However, placement is often misleading if a ✔ is used.

5. Use of Screens

Use screens and other visual aids to help guide the eyes, not as decorations. Screening can be very helpful on a form. The contrast of the shaded areas with the unshaded highlights both of them. The illustrations show how screening can be used to:

Separate areas on the form (Example 1)
Highlight areas that are not to be filled in or are to be filled in only by certain people (Examples 2 and 3)
Separate caption areas from fill-in spaces (Example 4)
Give the illusion of a colored background (Example 5)

EXAMPLE 1

CHARGE BACK	SPECIAL INSTRUCTIONS								
DO NOT CHARGE BACK	SHIP EXACT QUANTITY [ ]		POST DATED ORDER DO NOT SHIP BEFORE _____						
BACK ORDERED	SHIPPED	ORDERED	UNIT	UNIT PKG.	STOCK NUMBER				
A									
B									
C									
D									
E									
F									
G									
H									
I									
J									
K									
TOTAL PIECES		TOTAL WEIGHT							CHECKER

EXAMPLE 2

		Qty. ret'd. For test	Quantity Involved	Credit Req.	LAB USE Compl. Justified	M
				Y N	Y N O	
				Y N	Y N O	
				Y N	Y N O	
				Y N	Y N O	
				Y N	Y N O	
				Y N	Y N O	
				Y N	Y N O	
				Y N	Y N O	

EXAMPLE 3

DISTRIBUTION BY PROJECT (IF NECESSARY)

		PROJECT	AMOUNT

TR. ANALYSIS USE

oyee

EXAMPLE 4

SUMMARY		
CATEGORY		**AMOUNT**
Personal Car Allow		
Co. Car Gas	Gals	Cost
Parking and Tolls		
Taxi and Limo		
Room		
Meals		
Phone		
Miscellaneous		
Entertainment		
Air - RR Tickets		
Rental Car plus gas		
C o m p a n y C a r Accident Repairs		
Lub, Wash, Mech. Rpr.		
License		
Tire Repair		
SUB TOTAL		
Less Co. Car Pers. Miles @8¢ Per Mile		—
TOTAL EXPENSE		
RELOCATION ACCT. 6725		—
NET CASH EXPENSE		
AUTH. NO.		—
Balance Due Employee		
Balance Due Company		

CO. CAR ONLY

O D O M E T E R	Present	
	Prior	
M I L E A G E	Total	
	Business	
	Personal	

ADVANCE REPAYMENT
Enter Auth. No. + total amt., incl. tickets, from Travel Auth, Form 354. Attach copy of Authorization.

ATTACH CHECK OR RECEIPT FROM CASHIER ➤

EXAMPLE 5

CONVERTER—END USER
Name

Contact

City, State, Zip

CUSTOMER
Name

Contact

City, State, Zip

REFERENCE DATA

3M Invoice No.	Invoice Date	Customer P.O. No.	3M Sales Representative	Date Prepared

COMPLAINT MATERIAL

	Product Type & Description (Sheets, Rolls, Basis Wt.,CB,CFB,CF)	Lot Number	Sheet Size or Roll Width	Color
1				
2				
3				
4				
5				

In addition, screens can be used to indicate computer input fields.

Visual aids called dingbats are also used to draw attention to or highlight areas on a form. For example, an arrow or asterisk is often placed at the beginning of a signature box, expecially when the signer does not fill out the rest of the form.

Proper use of screening and dingbats does make the form look better. But it's more important that these devices be used to make the form *work* better.

6. Margins

Providing a proper margin, or unprinted area, on the form is very simple and very necessary. It is also frequently overlooked.

Margins are important for several reasons. First, printing presses generally do not print out to the edge of the piece of paper on all four sides. Presses require some space for "lockup" or "gripper." This is for the mechanism on the press cylinder that holds the printing plate in position. Obviously, there can be no printing in that space. If the layout does not allow an adequate margin, the printer may prepare an over-sized form that is cut down to the requested size. Or, the form may be printed using two plates, one of them covering the lockup area of the other. In either case, the extra expense of the time and effort involved will be charged to the purchaser.

Second, and more important, the form works better with a margin. If someone wants to bind the form in any type of binder or folder, a margin is absolutely required. If someone wants to make a copy of the form, it better have a margin or part of the data will be lost. If the form is going to be handled by people, as all forms are, it should have a margin to prevent fingers and thumbs from smearing the information entered on the form.

As a standard practice, allowing a ⅜″ margin all the way around the form is adequate. The size should be adjusted to accommodate any special requirements. For example, a normal three-ring punch needs at least ⅝″ on the side with the holes, but preferably ¾″ or 1″.

7. Make the Form Self-Instructing

If the form has been designed properly, there is little need for a detailed procedure explaining how to fill it out. A procedure manual should simply say, "Fill out Form 107." Any employee needing Form 107 should be able to fill it out with no other help. This applies especially to forms used by many people as an incidental part of their job. A high-volume form, such as an invoice or purchase order, should not require fill-in instructions on each form. But, even on these forms, there should be instructions and explanations to the people receiving them.

When writing instructions on the form, make them easy to understand. Just as with captions, instructions should be comprehensible by the new user who is not familiar with the system. But be careful not to over-explain simple items. Proper usage of the form and its part in the overall procedure must be clear, but explaining too much will insult the intelligence of most users. This will create a poor attitude toward the form and its designer.

EXAMPLE 6

Read the certificate at the end of this questionnaire before completing your answers. *Print* or *Type* all answers. All questions and statements must be completed. If proper answer is "no" or "none" so indicate. Fill out, sign, and return to requesting agency. If more space is required, use remarks section.

1. Read the certificate at the end of this questionnaire before completing your answers.

2. PRINT or TYPE all answers. All questions and statements, must be completed. If proper answer is "no" or "none," so indicate.

3. Fill out, sign, and return to requesting agency.

4. If more space is required, use remarks section.

Bear in mind that most people will not read the instructions. They will scan them, to spot anything of interest, but they will not study them. As shown in Example 6, an outline style is easier to scan than a paragraph format, so specific instructions are more likely to be noticed.

Be wary of printing instructions on the back of the form. Most people will not notice them—but, even if they do, few users will bother to turn the form over to read the instructions. Instructions on the backs of forms tend to become wordy. The designer tries to use up the space and often defines every caption that is shown on the front. The portion of a full page of back-printed instructions shown in Example 7 illustrates this fault.

If the form is a book or pad with an index card used as a barrier between sets, many of the instructions can be printed on the index card or on the cover of the book or pad, as shown in Example 8.

Instructions are most effective when they are included in the body of the form itself, close to the item that is being explained. (If the captions are well chosen, few will have to be explained any further.) The Travel Authorization (Example 9) is a carefully planned self-instructing form.

EXAMPLE 7

INSTRUCTIONS FOR COMPLETING EMPLOYEE STATUS CHANGE NOTICE

THIS FORM IS TO BE USED FOR ALL OTHER CHANGES THAT DO NOT INVOLVE A HIRE, REHIRE OR TERMINATED EMPLOYEE. THERE IS A SEPARATE FORM (COLOR DISTINCTION) WHICH IS TO BE USED FOR PARENT COMPANY VERSUS SUBSIDIARIES

TYPE OF PAYROLL ON WHICH
TO BE PAID: (INDICATE)

HOURLY — FACTORY HOURLY PRODUCTION WORKERS WHO ARE PAID ON A WEEKLY BASIS. THERE ARE A FEW INSTANCES WHERE SALES BRANCH OFFICE WAREHOUSE EMPLOYEES FALL INTO THIS CATEGORY. THESE ARE LOCATIONS WHERE THERE ARE PAYROLL DEDUCTIONS FOR UNION DUES.

BI-WEEKLY — BI-WEEKLY SALARIED EMPLOYEES PAID FOR TWO WEEKS ENDING ON A FRIDAY PAID THE FOLLOWING FRIDAY. THERE ARE INSTANCES WHERE SOME OF THE LOCATIONS REQUIRE THE PERSONNEL ON THIS TYPE OF PAYROLL TO BE PAID WEEKLY DUE TO LEGAL REQUIREMENTS.

SUPERVISOR'S NAME
PREVIOUS — THE EMPLOYEE'S PREVIOUS SUPERVISOR.

CURRENT — THE EMPLOYEE'S IMMEDIATE SUPERVISOR.

EFFECTIVE DATE OF CHANGE — THE DATE THE CHANGE BECOMES EFFECTIVE.

PERMANENT (INDICATE) — EMPLOYEES WHO ARE REGULARLY SCHEDULED TO 37½, OR 40 HOURS PER WEEK.

TEMPORARY (INDICATE) — EMPLOYEES WHO ARE AN EMERGENCY CIPAT

EXAMPLE 8

ALL C.S.O.'S MUST BE COMPLETED IN BALL POINT PEN AND MUST BE LEGIBLE.

A C.S.O. must be completed anytime you work on a unit, regardless of how small your involvement.

TYPE OF CALL

Place an 'X' in the box or boxes indicating the type of call. More than one box may be checked, but only the following combinations are acceptable:

'X' in Box No.	Description of Call
1	Installation of M-400, M-202 or M-20.
2	Emergency call, unit under P.M.A.
2,3	Emergency call, unit under P.M.A. and Scheduled inspection is performed.
2,4	Emergency call, unit under P.M.A., and last call was less than 30 days prior.
3	Scheduled inspection of P.M.A. unit.
5	Emergency call, unit is under warranty.
5,4	Emergency call, unit is under warranty and last call was less than 30 days ago.
6	Emergency call, unit is not under P.M.A., is not under warranty, and has not been serviced in past 30 days.
6,4	Emergency call, unit is not under P.M.A., is not under warranty, but last call was less than 30 days ago.

Note 1: Box No. 4 is never the only box checked. A 30-day recall indicates that the unit involved was serviced within the past 30 days only. You must also indicate whether it is a P.M.A., WARRANTY, or CHARGE unit.

PROBLEM COMPONENT

This box is never left blank. One of five possible entries will always be made:

- A. An 11 digit 3M part number
- B. SCH PMA
- C. IN STAL
- D. CND
- E. CUST EROR

In the case of an emergency call, enter the part number of the specific component which failed and caused the unit to malfunction. If more than one component has failed, enter the part number of the one most responsible for generating the call.

If, during an installation, a component fails and causes a machine malfunction, or is serviced because you feel it would certainly cause a machine malfunction, enter the part number of that component here.

If, while performing a scheduled P.M.A. inspection, a component is serviced because it is about to fail and that component is not in the tune-up kit, enter the part number of that component here.

If no problems are found while performing a scheduled P.M.A. inspection, enter SCH PMA here.
NEVER ENTER THE PART NUMBER OF A P.M.A. KIT IN THIS BOX.

If no problems are found during an installation, enter IN STAL here.

There appears to be an increase in the number of calls where the problem cannot be discovered and no malfunction is noted. When this occurs, and the problem cannot be traced to a specific component or to customer error, the new write-in category, CND, allows you to report that you COULD NOT DUPLICATE the malfunction. You should use this write-in only after thoroughly troubleshooting the unit.

If customer error generated the service call, enter CUST EROR.

CUSTOMER SERVICE ORDER

Type of Call:	Date Serviced	Model	Serial Number	Service Rep.
☐ 1 - Installation	2 4 78	2 0 0	2 6 1 1 - 0 4 9 5	X X - 0 1
☐ 2 - PMA-Emer.	Problem Component			Cycles since Problem Comp. Last serviced.
☐ 3 - PMA-Schd	1 2 - 2 3 7 6 - 0 0 9 4 - 0			3 0 0
☐ 4 - 30 Day Recall	NUMBER OF CYCLES SINCE UNIT WAS LAST SERVICED. 2 2 5	DATE UNIT WAS LAST SERVICED. 10 1 77 Mo. Day Yr.		Service Order No.
☐ 5 - Warranty	DISPOSITION OF PROBLEM COMPONENT	COUNTER READING		
☒ 6 - Charge	☐ Repaired ☒ Replaced	IN 750 / 755 OUT S 2 3 T 1 8		

Customer Order Number	Order Date	Invoice Number	Terms
S-4567	2-4-78		NET

CUSTOMER	CHARGE TO
Name SICKLY HOSPITAL	Name (If other than customer) SICKLY HOSPITAL
Address 1000 CRESTVIEW ROAD	Address P.O. BOX #901
City-State-Zip WELLSVILLE, USA 94040	City-State-Zip WELLSVILLE, USA 94040

DESCRIPTION OF WORK PERFORMED	QUAN.	PART NUMBER	PRICE	AMOUNT
REPLACE VACUUM PUMP	1	12 2376 0094 0	320.00	320 00
REPLACE CHECK VALVE	1	12 2376 0073 4	91.00	91 00
REPLACE VACUUM GAUGE	1	12 2376 0092 4	40.00	40 00
REPLACE MANIFOLD GASKET	1	12 2376 0040 3	3.20	3 20
REPLACE MYLAR WASHER	1	12 2376 0041 1	2.15	2 15
REPLACE DOOR LATCH	1	12 2376 0024 7	15.10	15 10
INSTALL TUNE UP KIT		12 2376 1213 5	98.60	98 60
PERFORMED LEAK TEST - NO				
LEAKS DETECTED.				
CHECKED ALL UNITS FUNCTIONS				

Comments			
Complaints WON'T DRAW VACUUM + DOOR FALLS OPEN.		TOTAL PARTS ▶	570 05
		4% State/Local Tax	22 80
Problem PUMP DEFECTIVE, DOOR	Labor Charge 3 Hrs. @ $ 40.00 Per Hour		120 00
LATCH WORN.	Travel Charge 2 Hrs. @ $ 40.00 Per Hour		80 00
Solution REPLACED BOTH	☐ Unit is covered by PMA; however, the labor and travel charge on this call is outside the terms of the agreement.		
	PMA Labor and Travel Hrs. @ $ ___ Per Hour		
	Customer Signature Miss Brock Date	SUB TOTAL ▶	792 85
Service Representative Signature John Q. Service Date 2/4/78		TOTAL CHARGES ▶	792 85

Form 12846-C

CHARGE TO

If the customer has a separate/special billing address, please enter the name and address in the charge to area.

COMMENT SECTION

Complaint — — — Enter a brief description of the customer complaint if the customer generated the call. If you generated the call, enter NONE.

Problem — — — Enter a brief description of the actual problem(s) you discovered while servicing the unit.

Solution — — — Enter a brief description of the corrective action(s) you took while servicing the unit. Also enter any general comments regarding the condition of the unit, installation problems, operator problems, etc.

Your comments should be brief but accurate and in no way derogatory toward the customer. No personal remarks should be made on any C.S.O. which reflect your feelings about the equipment or the customer. Report facts only on the C.S.O.

PMA LABOR & TRAVEL

If a unit is under PMA but the current call falls outside the terms of a PMA for any reason, labor and travel charges apply. Place check mark in box and enter charges in space provided.

EXAMPLE 9

TRAVEL AUTHORIZATION

Auth. No. **664223**

Enter this number on expense voucher, line 29

Use to request all advance funds and, in St. Paul, to obtain transportation tickets from Travel Planning.

	Name		Empl. No.	Dept. No.	Phone
Employee					

Purpose of Trip/Advance	

General Itinerary -Show dates and both originating city & destination	

Mode of Travel

Air Tourist ☐	Train ☐	Plane ☐	Car ☐	Air First Class ☐ ◄— approval ——►	First Class O.K. (Treasurer or Div. Head)	Date

Advance Needed
-in St. Paul, do not include cost of tickets

Amount $	Type ☐ Temporary ☐ Permanent	Cash ☐	Check ☐ ◄— mail to ——►	
SHOW "NONE" IF NOT APPLICABLE				

Approvals
-If Dept Head is also auth. signer, use Auth. block

Dept. Head	Date	Authorization	Date	Cashier Use Only

Receipt
-sign only when you receive the cash or ticket, not before

CASH	Received from Cashier in Building _____		Amount $	Received by	Date
TICKET	Ticket Number		Amount $	Received by	Date
				◄Show "NONE" if not applicable	
Total Temp. Advance	Total of cash or check advance plus cost of ticket.		$ .00	◄Enter this amount on your Expense Voucher, Line 30.	

To get cash — bring approved set to Cashier

To get check — send approved original to Travel Advance

Branch use — bring set to Manager for working fund draft

— for branch use —	
Send original white copy to Travel Advance. Send the canary copy with A/P draft copy. Attach pink to Branch copy.	Draft No.
	Amount $

Original White — Advance control   Canary — Ticket control   Pink — supervisor   Gold— Attach to Exp. Voucher   White Copy — Employee

Federal tax returns are also good examples of self-instructing forms. The instructions are included both in the format and in a separate accompanying booklet. Most people, if they are patient and careful, can follow the instructions and prepare their own tax return, even though the laws and regulations are very complicated. (Many of you have probably never thought of your tax return as a well-designed form before. This illustrates very emphatically how important the user's attitude is toward the form and its related system: We don't like to pay taxes, so we don't like the forms.)

8. Distribution and Routing Information

The person who has filled out a form has to know what to do with it. Should it be mailed, delivered, or filed? The recipient should know who else has the same information. A procedure manual cannot take care of this. People don't keep open manuals on their desks. In most cases, they're locked up in the boss's office, unavailable to the forms users. The distribution information should appear on the form itself.

This information can be shown in various ways, all of them effective. It can be included in the instructions on the form, spread across the bottom, or stacked on the bottom (see Example 10 for illustrations of all three methods). It can also be shown as marginal words. In this case, only the routing for that one part is shown on each part.

Generally, if the form is printed by a forms manufacturer, you'll use marginal words. This feature won't cost anything extra and will get the job done. Depending on the manufacturer, there are certain size limitations and area limitations for this printing. Usually, it's done in red ink.

If the form is being printed in house, use the spread or stacked distribution. It is incorporated in the single plate used for all parts and

EXAMPLE 10

Send white copy of Request and suggested layout to: FORMS ADMINISTRATION

Keep canary copy for your record. On new forms, you will receive a copy of the specification sheet as confirmation.

White — Customer
Canary — Distributor
Pink — Sales Manager
Gold — Sales Representative

— or —

White — Customer   Canary — Distributor   Pink — Sales Manager is an economical, effective way to show routing. However, this method does require colored paper for identification of the various parts. I prefer the spread or stacked method for all forms. It provides more information to the users, which in turn improves the effectiveness of the form.

9. Form Number and Title

Whenever anyone picks up a form, that person has a right to know what it is. Forms are identified by a title and a number. Form numbers are used for inventory control, for ordering, for reference in written procedures, and for identification within a forms administration function. (See Chapter 8 for a detailed discussion of the different types of numbering systems.) Regardless of the system, the number should be shown on the form.

Form numbers have appeared in almost every possible spot on the form. I have seen them in the lower left corner, lower right corner, upper right corner, and the upper left corner. This seems to be a matter of personal preference and style. I prefer the upper left location, along with the company identification and form title. Our reading habits take us to the upper left to start reading. It makes sense to tell the readers right away what they are reading. And, if the filing reference is in the upper right corner (as is normally the case), the upper left is usually not used for fill-in data. So it's a good spot for identification and also for basic instructions, as shown in Example 11.

When selecting a title, make sure it is significant and meaningful to those who will be using it. The title should clearly indicate the pur-

EXAMPLE 11

REQUEST FOR FORM

FORM

	TRAVEL EXPENSE VOUCHER		EMP
	FORM		
HOME ADDRESS (City, State, Zip)			E
	ITINERARY		
DATE	FROM INTERMEDIATE	TO	

pose of the form. The list of title keys shown here will help develop good titles on your forms. In most cases, including the word "form" in the title is not advisable.

FORM TITLE KEYS	
Key Word	*Action or Decision*
Acknowledgment	to document the receipt of
Affidavit	to attest to the truth of
Agreement	to offer and accept in writing
Appeal	to request a review
Application	to request something
Authorization	to permit something
Award	to bestow, to grant, to give
Bid	to offer for a price
Bill	to itemize
Cancellation	to revoke
Claim	to ask as due
Communication	to interchange information
Complaint	to allege, to report a problem
Contract	to agree to provide for a price
Deed	to convey real estate
Digest	to classify and condense
Endorsement	to assign
Estimate	to calculate approximately
Follow-up	to seek completion of an action
Guide	to direct the course
Identification	to name
Index	to list
Inquiry	to seek to know
Instruction	to furnish with direction
Invoice	to bill or charge for
Itinerary	to record a trip, usually in advance
Journal	to record daily transactions and status
Lease	to rent
Ledger	to record accounting data
List	to catalog or itemize
Log	to record individual actions
Manifest	to list cargo or shipments
Memorandum	to record informally
Message	to communicate
Note	to assist the memory, to acknowledge a debt

FORM TITLE KEYS (cont.)	
Key Word	*Action or Decision*
Notice	to announce information or directions
Notification	to formally send information
Order	to command, to requisition
Pass	to permit to go and come
Permit	to authorize a specific action
Petition	to request formally
Questionnaire	to ask questions to obtain data
Receipt	to acknowledge delivery or payment
Recommendation	to advise on course of action
Record	to retain an account of facts or events
Register	to list events or actions in sequence
Release	to set free, to allow shipment
Report	to make an account of action or status
Request	to ask for
Requisition	to ask that something be supplied
Roll	to register events or names
Roster	to list names
Routing	to direct materials from one place to another
Schedule	to list recurring events, to publish a plan of future actions
Specification	to state requirements
Statement	to communicate a declaration or report, to summarize invoices
Summary	to contain the substance of a fuller account
Survey	to inspect, to examine and report
Tabulation	to arrange in a systematic outline
Ticket	to attach to goods giving identification information, to give the holder specified privileges
Transcript	to provide a written copy
Transmittal	to send out an attachment
Voucher	to bear witness, receipt for payment

10. Overall Use of Lines and Words

All lines and words on the form should guide the entry, interpretation, and use of information. This tenth commandment is a summary of the other nine, which outline specific ways to accomplish this purpose. It is also a warning to every forms designer: You and I can become so engrossed in following the rules and standards that we lose sight of our objective.

Our objective is not to apply these standards to every form, it is to provide the best possible tool for the users. The standards are a guide to help design better forms; they are not an end in themselves. It is possible to follow every standard and still produce an unusable or ineffective form—but that should never happen.

STEP-BY-STEP DESIGN METHOD

Let's apply the basic techniques of forms design that we've been discussing. If you go through the step-by-step process that follows, you will probably come up with an acceptable form. (You will find that many layouts will be acceptable but probably none will be perfect.) Keep in mind that ten people designing the same form will undoubtedly produce ten different layouts.

Sort Out Information

Usually, the first step is to arrange the information into groups and then decide on the arrangement of those groups on the form. Some of the information groups that you will find include:

Key information. This is what will be used to reference or find the document, such as a serial number or a customer's name. It should be located so that it is easily visible. Many times, the most logical place for the key is the upper right corner. Don't put it there every time though; placement depends on how the document is to be filed and retrieved.

Instructions. These, too, should be conspicuous. Usually, the best place is at the upper left corner or alongside the area of the form where they are needed.

Supplemental data. Tables, lists, reference codes, or explanations can normally be placed at the bottom of the form or, if space is not available, on the back of the form.

Body. This is the information that is being transmitted. It will take up most of the space and, in many cases, can be broken up into groups for easier use and understanding.

Approvals. These are the signature boxes and so on that signify someone's approval of the action requested or the information presented. They usually appear at the bottom of the form, but remember that they may be located elsewhere if that would make the form work better.

Sample Design Problem

To illustrate this process, let's go through a design exercise together. Your personnel department wants to have a card for each employee that contains information needed by various people. They will be filing the cards in a "recipe" box. The size of each card is 8″ wide by 5″ high.

The cards will be completed by the personnel department secretary on a standard typewriter (six lines per inch), and will be filed and referenced by that same secretary. The personnel department expects to use about 1,000 cards per year.

The following information must be asked for (numbers in parentheses indicate number of digits):

Employee name   Department name
Street address   Department number (4)
City, state, Zip code   Supervisor's name
Home telephone   Supervisor's office phone
Office telephone   Job title   ⎫
Emergency contact   Salary group (2)   ⎬ Room for
Emergency contact's phone   Monthly salary (4) ⎪ original entry
Employee number (4)   Effective date   ⎭ and two changes
Social Security number (11)

Our first step is to identify logical groups this information falls into. With some study of the requested data, we find these groups:

Name and address
Emergency contact data
Company information
Job information
Employee reference numbers
Form identification

EXAMPLE 12

Name And Address

Emergency Contact

Company Info

Job Info

Title And Number

Employee No.
Soc Sec No.

Home Telephone

Example 12 shows an arrangement of these groups of information. You may be able to plan this mentally—but even if you don't need to write it down, you must be sure to do it in some way.

In our example the cards will be filed by employee name. That is the *key* data and is located in the most visible spot for the type of filing system used. In a recipe box file, the cards stand upright. When searching the file, most people use their right hand to finger through the cards, leaving the upper left corner of the card visible. Hence, the employee name has been placed in the upper left corner. (If the secretary is left-handed, consider placing key information in the upper right corner.)

Example 13 shows the results of arranging each data field within the previously arranged groups. It is important to develop a logical sequence. Note the name and address group. The sequence shown is the one that people normally use for this data. It would be ineffective to ask for the street address first, then the name, and finally, the city, state, and Zip code. Also, people are accustomed to using three or four lines to fill in their address (that's how it appears on a letter). Asking for it in a different arrangement will be less effective. (Although not illustrated by this problem, it's important to consider the setup of another document that will be referred to when people fill out the form you are designing, and the arrangement of information on subsequent documents. This is extremely critical on computer input forms, but important on all others as well.)

The next step is allocating the right amount of space for each data field. Using the 3-by-5 principle for vertical spacing, Example 14 shows how much room is provided for each entry. The lines have been arranged so that the typist can always use the carriage return lever set on double-space. As you will see, however, this layout does not look very good. It's not balanced and there is a lot of "wasted" space.

Go on to Example 15 which shows the result of adjusting space allocation to make the form work better. The adjusted layout will be easier to type on and to read, and it looks more balanced. We have made good use of the extra space available.

All of these steps have been planning steps. Now we can start to make a layout. Layouts should be done to exact size and should look as much like the finished form as possible. The form user should be able to look at the layout and approve it without seeing the camera-ready artwork. Likewise, the compositor, when preparing the artwork,

EXAMPLE 13

Name   Employee No.
Street Address   Social Security No.
City, State, Zip   Home Phone

Emergency Contact Name, Relationship, Telephone

Department Name, Dept. No.   Office Phone
Supervisor Name   Supv. Phone

Job Title   Salary Group   Monthly Salary   Date
1   1   1   1
2   2   2   2
3   3   3   3

Title
Number

EXAMPLE 14

EXAMPLE 15

should not have to make any assumptions about or adjustments to your layout. That could foul up the spacing requirements that you worked so hard to develop and might make the form unusable.

To minimize the use of my eraser and to save a lot of redrawing, I have found it helpful to first draw all horizontal lines as shown in Example 16. It's easy to make mistakes on these lines, and corrections or redrawing are much simpler if the vertical lines and captions haven't been inserted. You can also make one last check to see that the vertical space has been properly allocated before completing the layout.

Next, draw in the vertical lines to form the individual boxes and groups of boxes (see Example 17). Now you can check the total layout for accuracy and efficiency before spending a lot of time printing in the captions.

Once the layout is correct as far as the lines are concerned, insert all the captions, titles, and instructions (see Example 18). Show the words as you want them to appear on the finished form. If you want both capital and small letters, show them that way. Also, write as close as possible to the size that you expect. If you don't do this, the user will not be able to approve your layout, as it will not look like the form will look.

Now the layout needs to be approved by the user. It is advisable to give the user several copies of the layout for testing to see that it will work. Don't give out your original layout for review. If you're lucky enough to get it back, it will probably have marks all over it.

Your layout will probably not be accepted as-is the first time. Be surprised and pleased if it is approved, but don't be disappointed if the user wants to make changes. In fact, you should encourage users to review the layout carefully. They should understand that their approval of the pencil layout is their final approval. In most cases, it is not necessary or advisable for the users to proofread the camera-ready artwork. That's the analyst's job. If the layout was prepared well, the user does not need to see the proof to know what the form will be like.

Once the layout has been approved, the basic design work is complete. But the analyst's work is not finished. Specifications must be written, purchasing and production must be arranged, the job must be discussed with the supplier in some cases, the artwork must be proofread, and a sample of the completed forms must be examined.

EXAMPLE 16

EXAMPLE 17

EXAMPLE 18

Employee Name		Employee Number		
Street Address		Social Security Number		
City, State, Zip		Home Telephone		

| Emergency Contact Name | | Relation | Emergency Telephone |

| Department Name | | Dept. No. | Office Telephone |
| Supervisor Name | | | Supv. Office Telephone |

Job Title		Salary Group	Mon. Salary	Effective Date

EMPLOYEE INFORMATION RECORD
FORM 8910

Selecting Type and Lines

What type style should we use? How large or small should it be? How thin or wide should the lines be? What kind of lines should we use? Your choices will have a definite effect on the efficiency and the value of the tools you design.

In answering these questions, remember the tenth commandment of forms layout: All lines and words on the form should guide the entry, interpretation, and use of information. We should be very concerned about the appearance of the form after it has been filled in. After all, it's the data that is added to the form that we're primarily concerned with. The preprinted form itself is only an aid to get the fill-in data. Don't ever get that confused.

Choosing Styles of Type

There are thousands of different typefaces in existence. How do we select one for our form?

We want one that is easy to read
We want one that is simple and plain
We want one that is uniform and standard
We want one that is nice in appearance

These general standards will help ensure (1) that the forms are easy for the originator to understand, (2) that the information added to the form is more prominent than the printed captions, (3) that the form looks nice, and (4) that a number of forms manufacturers could produce the artwork and the form.

Example 19 shows two major styles of type: *serif* and *sans serif*. As you can see, the sans serif style is all business. There are no flourishes on the ends of each line as there are on the serif letters and numbers. All the lines are the same width, in contrast to the varying widths of lines in the serif type.

In the small sizes normally used on forms, sans serif is easy to read and then it seems to recede into the background after the data has been entered. It is a standard style of type that is available throughout the printing industry. It fits our requirements for a typeface better than the serif style. I have found the Univers style to be one that works well on forms.

77

EXAMPLE 19

10 PT. UNIVERS UN-10-M

"IF YOU WORK FOR A MAN, IN HEAVEN'S NAME WORK FOR HIM, SPEAK WELL OF HIM, AND STAND BY THE INSTITUTION HE REPRESENTS. "REMEMBER, AN OUNCE OF LOYALTY IS WORTH A POUND OF CLEVERNESS." "If you must growl, condemn and eternally find fault, resign your position and when you are on the outside, damn to your heart's content... But as long as you are a part of the institution, do not condemn it. If you do, the first high wind that

* 1 2 3 4 5 6 7 8 9 0 *

10 PT. CENTURY C-10-M

"IF YOU WORK FOR A MAN, IN HEAVEN'S NAME WORK FOR HIM, SPEAK WELL OF HIM, AND STAND BY THE INSTITUTION HE REPRESENTS. "REMEMBER, AN OUNCE OF LOYALTY IS WORTH A POUND OF CLEVERNESS." "If you must growl, condemn and eternally find fault, resign your position and when you are on the outside, damn to your heart's content... But as long as you

* 1 2 3 4 5 6 7 8 9 0 *

However, for blocks of copy such as lengthy instructions or contract clauses, a serif style is the most readable. Because of the varied line widths, and the flourishes on each character, our eyes recognize the characters and words faster and easier—when reading sentences, paragraphs, and full pages. That is also why this style is usually used for books and magazines.

To emphasize or highlight words or phrases, several things can be done with type styles. You can use *italics*, which is basically a slanted version of the typeface. Or, you can use a **boldface** type, which looks darker on the form. Both these styles draw attention because they are different. A word of caution is necessary, however; excessive use of either destroys the attention-getting quality and makes a form very difficult to read.

After selecting the typeface, you have to decide whether to use all capital letters (uppercase) or to use both capital and small letters (upper- and lowercase). Most forms use uppercase letters for captions and upper- and lowercase for instructions and other large blocks of copy. This is what you should expect to get from a forms manufacturer if you do not specify something else.

As a general rule, using all uppercase letters, as shown in Example 20, is satisfactory for high-volume forms, which are generally machine generated. They have been standard for years, so manufacturers are accustomed to working with them. Captions on computer output forms are seldom read, but are there if needed. Lines can be printed close together because you do not have to allow for ascenders and descenders.

On handwritten or typed forms, however, where the captions are usually read prior to completing the form, I prefer to use both upper- and lowercase letters. Words written that way are easier to read because of the varied size of the letters. As most forms in any organization will be filled in manually, the standard decision should probably be to use both upper- and lowercase letters (see Example 21).

Points and Picas

Another question to be answered concerns the size of the type. How small should it be? How large? You may not be familiar with points and picas, which are units of measurement used by printers. A point is equal to *about* $1/72''$; a pica is made up of 12 points and is equal to *about* $1/6''$. The "about" in each case is very important. Nearly all composition equipment is set up to space in point increments. It is

EXAMPLE 20

EXAMPLE 21

Form Title			Form Number
			— —
Release No.	Date Ordered	Date Needed	Quantity Ordered

This order is for:

☐ Exact Reprint - proof not required

☐ Revised Form - ⎰ Submit proof to

☐ New Form   - ⎱ Forms Administration

For copy, see:

☐ Sample attached

☐ Forms Administration

☐ Carbon Test Required

☐ Continuous   Printer: _____   Other: _____

Marginal punches: ☐ Yes   ☐ No

Marginal perf.   :   ☐ No   ☐ Left _____"   ☐ Right _____"

Marginal fastening:

Glue   L   R

Easy release glue   L   R

Crimp only   L   R

Crimp, with   L   R

  Easy release glue

EXAMPLE 22

24 points   1/3 inch

impossible to space lines ⅓″ apart using points. The variance accumulates as you go down a page, rendering a form with lines drawn by a compositor unusable on a typewriter. Likewise, layout sheets with point spacing are unusable for forms layout work. (This is shown in Example 22.) You probably wonder why printers and compositors continue using such an archaic measurement system when it does not fit the requirements of users of the paperwork they produce. So do I. But the situation does exist and we have to coexist with it.

When used to designate type size, the number of points indicates the approximate height of the letters, from the bottom of the descender on one to the top of the ascender on another. Generally, we can figure that the number of lines per inch will be 72 divided by the point size. As an example, there would be six lines of 12-point type in 1″, ten lines of 7-point, and so on. But remember *not* to use 12 points as ⅙″, or 24 points as ⅓″—you're in trouble if you do.

When using upper- and lowercase letters, a 7-point size is very good for captions within the boxes. If only uppercase letters are used, a 6-point size is adequate. Smaller sizes are difficult to read, especially for older people. Larger sizes are too big for upper left caption placement without using valuable fill-in space, and tend to dominate the fill-in data rather than recede into the background.

For instructions, 8-point Univers italics works quite well. Instructions are not usually within a fill-in box, so the larger size is not a

EXAMPLE 23

7 PT. UNIVERS   UN-7-M

"IF YOU WORK FOR A MAN, IN HEAVEN'S NAME WORK FOR HIM, SPEAK WELL OF HIM, AND STAND BY THE INSTITUTION HE REPRESENTS. "REMEMBER, AN OUNCE OF LOYALTY IS WORTH A POUND OF CLEVERNESS." "If you must growl, condemn and eternally find fault, resign your position and when you are on the outside, damn to your heart's content... But as long as you are a part of the institution, do not condemn it. If you do, the first high wind that comes along will blow you away and probably you will never know why."

8 PT. UNIVERS   UN-8-MI

"IF YOU WORK FOR A MAN, IN HEAVEN'S NAME WORK FOR HIM, SPEAK WELL OF HIM, AND STAND BY THE INSTITUTION HE REPRESENTS. "REMEMBER, AN OUNCE OF LOYALTY IS WORTH A POUND OF CLEVERNESS." "If you must growl, condemn and eternally find fault, resign your position and when you are on the outside, damn to your heart's content... But as long as you are a part of the institution, do not condemn it. If you do, the first high wind that comes along will blow you away and probably you will never know why."

space-waster. And it is not so large that it looks out of place next to the 7-point caption. For major headings and for the form title, a 10-point type works well. The headings and titles, while more obvious, are not overstated and garish. Samples of different type sizes are shown in Example 23.

Lines or Rules

The lines or rules on a form perform a variety of functions. Some guide our eyes, some slow us down, others force us to stop writing or reading. They might be compared with the green, yellow, and red lights on a traffic signal. The thin rules, called hairlines (see Example 24), correspond to green lights. Most lines on a form will be of this

EXAMPLE 24

Company Car No.			Dept. No.	Dept. Name		Bldg-Fl.	Date
CAR INFO.	Year	Make		License No.		Parking Space No.	Time Promised
Other				Phone		Mileage	Driver (Sign)

kind. They help us write in a straight line and guide our eyes across or down the page. A slightly wider line (Example 25) is like the yellow light: It warns us that something different follows. These ½-point rules are used to separate areas on a form. Bold lines (Example 26) are the red lights. We really notice these 3-point rules. They are used to draw our attention to an area, or to begin or end major sections of the form. Double lines (parallel hairlines) create an effect similar to bold lines. (See Example 27.)

Broken lines, often called dotted lines, help guide our eyes when used horizontally. Vertically, they usually indicate the separation between dollars and cents, or they show an optional division of a field (Example 28).

Handwritten forms will normally have more lines than machine-generated forms. People need guidelines to indicate a definite area in which to write. Computers don't need writing lines or vertical columnar lines. After the computer output has been added to the form, it tends to develop its own tabulated columns and lines. If there is enough "white space," only a few lines are needed on these output forms.

EXAMPLE 25

Usage
Describe purpose, distribution, filing, retention, and disposition of each copy of form

Preparation
Indicate how the form will be filled out and the quantities to be used

SOURCE	☐ Multiple locations	☐ Single location *(specify)* (See Mailing Address below)	
PERSONNEL	☐ Clerical	☐ Production	☐ Other *(specify)*
METHOD	☐ Handwriting	☐ Typewriter	☐ Other *(specify)*

VOLUME USED	Quantity	Units ☐ Ea. ☐ Pads ☐ Bks.	Period ☐ Wk. ☐ Mo~ ☐

Suggested Specifications
Fill in if known.

ORDER QUANTITY	Quantity	Units	Mailing Address (sin~~
SIZE	Width	Heigh~	
NO. PAR~~			

EXAMPLE 26

NAME (FIRST LINE)						B/L COPIES
NAME (SECOND LINE)						
ADDRESS						INV. COPIES
CITY AND STATE				ZIP CODE		
SIC CODE	CLASS.	MAINT.	HDLG.	MAIL	BR. CR.	ACCOUNT NUMBER

EXAMPLE 27

_____ ...un. ⎕ Yr.

....ye user forms are not stocked at Bldg. 216)

		⎕ All White ⎕ Colors	Charge Code (for non-stock forms)	Date Needed
PAPER	⎕ Bond ⎕ Carbonless	⎕ Other	Requested by	Date
CONSTRUCTION	⎕ Sheets ⎕ Sets	⎕ Pads ⎕ Books	Department Name	Dept. No.
	⎕ Continuous		3M Address	3M Phone
PRE-NUMBERING	⎕ Yes, start with: ⎕ No		Approved by (Dept. Head) ▶	Date

Attach drawing of form, showing any additional specifications.

Forms Administration will write the final specs.

EXAMPLE 28

SERVICE PERFORMED

Project	Amount	(✓)	Service						Project	Amount
200			GAS Reg. ⎕ Prem. ⎕ No Lead ⎕ Gal. _____						100	
203			CHASSIS LUBRICATION						300	
203			CAR APPEARANCE ⎕ Exterior ⎕ Interior ⎕ Wax						400	
204			TIRE SERVICE	Left Front	Left Rear	Right Front	Right Rear	Spare		
204			⎕ Rotate ⎕ Mount						600	
601			⎕ Repair ⎕ Balance							
			LABOR						850	
800										

FORMS DESIGN CHECKLIST

After analyzing the intended use of the form and designing the appropriate tool, it's a good idea to review what has been done to make sure the form will work properly.

The individual pieces of information asked for on the rough layout or other documentation supplied by the user must be compared with the finished layout to make sure nothing was accidentally omitted. (I once worked many hours over a period of months on a very complex form, a notification of salary changes for employees temporarily assigned to work outside the United States. During the final check of the camera-ready copy, I discovered that the effective date of the increase was not on the form. I had erroneously omitted it from an earlier pencil layout, and yet the layouts had been approved through all stages by the user.)

After verifying that all the data elements are included, use the questions listed below as a checklist to determine whether or not the form has been well-designed. (These questions serve as reminders of techniques, rather than explanations of them.)

If any question is answered "no," that aspect of the design should be reviewed to see if further improvements can be made.

Arrangement
1. Are all items, and groups of items, arranged in the right sequence, considering the source of the information, its use, and the way users normally write or read it?
2. If the key information (that data used to retrieve the form from a file) in the most visible location, considering the type of filing equipment used?

Spacing
3. Is the proper amount of space provided for each piece of information requested, considering the preparation method?
4. Is the horizontal spacing adjusted to provide a minimum number of typewriter tab stops?
5. Is the vertical spacing set so that the typist can always use the carriage return lever or the key to move the carriage to the next line?
6. Is all extra space used properly for emphasis, separation, and balance rather than looking leftover?

Captions

7. Will all captions be understood by everyone who might use the form?
8. Are captions placed in the upper left corner of each fill-in area?
9. Will abbreviations be readily understood?
10. Are group captions or headings used to identify major areas?

Multiple Choice Answers

11. Are possible answers given whenever they would help the users provide better answers in less time?
12. Are the answers and check boxes arranged properly for the most productive and accurate fill-in?

Instructions and Distribution

13. Can someone unfamiliar with the form complete it without referring to any other source for help?
14. Have all unnecessary instructions and explanations been left off the form, so that the user's intelligence will not be insulted?
15. Are the distribution instructions shown on the form in the most effective way for its usage pattern and construction?
16. If an interior part is removed from the set before the others, is it slightly longer so it can be easily identified and removed?
17. Is the self-mailer format used whenever applicable?
18. Is the form designed to fit a window envelope whenever appropriate?

Margins

19. Does the form have adequate margins for the required lock-up (gripper) space on the press?
20. Are the margins adequate for any binding technique to be used, such as hole punches for notebooks and post-hole binders?
21. Are the margins adequate for other handling characteristics, such as filing, copying, stapling, and so on?

Type, Lines, and Screens

22. Do all of the lines on the form do what they are supposed to do? (Some guide, some separate, some stop.)
23. Is screening (shading) used where helpful to separate, highlight, or identify fields or zones, not just to decorate the form?
24. Within the same typeface, is there variation in the size of type, its boldness, and use of capital and small letters and italics to enhance the appearance and legibility of the form?

Construction

25. Is the size appropriate for both the printer and all users?
26. Is the construction right for the way the form will be handled?
27. Is the paper right for the form's use and retention needs?

28. Is the color of ink appropriate?
29. Are all appropriate holes, perforations, scores, etc. shown on the layout and not interfered with by the copy?

Identification

30. Is the title meaningful?
31. Is the form properly identified with a number for ease in referencing, ordering, inventorying, and so on?
32. Is the organization properly identified?

General

33. Will this form accomplish its purpose with the minimum amount of effort by all users?
34. Is this the best possible tool to do this job?

FORMS HANDLING ANALYSIS

The handling or processing factors listed in Table 2 cover most of the normal activities needed for processing forms. These should be taken into account when the form is designed. They are intended to be used to compare the required times for processing different forms. Although they are based on accepted work measurement principles and in some cases on actual time tests, these factors should not be used for measuring or evaluating the productivity of an individual or group.

The timing for typing elements is based on an output of 30 words per minute, which is typical for forms preparation. The point factors are based on a value of "1" for a single typed character or space. This makes it easy to compute the number of points needed to prepare a form and to compare that total with the figure for another form. To determine the points needed, use a sample form. Indicate on the form the points applicable for each operation. (Some people prefer using a separate analysis sheet for this computation, but that means writing all of the captions and actions on the analysis form.)

The first three operations listed can be considered as make-ready and cleanup work for preparation of the form. They include the steps needed to get the form into the typewriter and adjusted to the first typing position, and steps to remove the form after typing is completed and to remove the stub from the set. The first operation does not include setting margins or tabulator stops. Making these settings is included in the second operation. For timing a batch of forms, the second

Table 2. Forms handling analysis.

Operation	Time (seconds)	Points	Cost (cents)
Pick up multiple-part set, insert in typewriter, align, set at starting position, remove from typewriter, and separate parts	28.0	70	4.70
Same as above, but also set margins and tabs	48.0	120	8.04
With single sheets, add carbon and additional sheet to make set (for each additional part add this to above factors)	9.0	22	1.47
Typing elements			
Type one character or use space bar	.4	1	.07
Use shift key for capital letter	.8	2	.13
Use tabulator key for horizontal movement	1.2	3	.20
Use carriage return key or lever	2.4	6	.40
Adjust platen one line	2.4	6	.40
Adjust horizontal position	4.0	10	.67
Adjust horizontal and vertical positions	6.4	16	1.07
Type name and address (three lines)	19.0	48	3.22
Type name and address on envelope (complete)	30.0	75	5.03
Handwriting elements			
Print one character	.8	2	.13
Move to next field	1.6	4	.27
Move to next line	2.4	6	.40
Print a date	9.5	24	1.60
Print a name	14.6	36	2.41
Copying elements			
Go to copier 25 steps away, make two copies, return to work station (no waiting or wasted copies)	114.0	285	19.10
Add to above for each additional copy	3.0	8	.53
Read data on one sheet prior to entering on another (per word or number)	1.2	3	.20
Verify fill-in data (per word or number)	3.2	8	.54
Post or record on log or register (per word or number)	9.5	24	1.61
Sort and file 20 documents	600.0	1,500	100.50
Add for each additional document	27.0	68	4.56
Fold and insert sheet in envelope	18.0	45	3.02
Open envelope, remove and unfold sheet	14.0	36	2.41
Moisten and apply gummed label	20.0	50	3.35
Apply pressure-sensitive label, with peel-off liner	15.0	38	2.54

88

function would be used for the first form and the first function for all following transactions.

If multiple parts are needed but not provided as part of the form, the factors for the third operation must be added to both of the first two factors. This is the time required to add carbons and extra sheets to a single-sheet original. It is apparent that the labor costs of almost 1.5¢ per part make this process of assembling multiple-part sets much more expensive than providing multiple-part unit sets.

The various typing factors are generally self-explanatory. In using them, be sure to account for every movement of the typewriter from the first typing position to the last character typed. The same is true of the handwriting elements.

The copying factors include getting up from the desk, walking to a copier 25 steps away, making two copies with no waiting or waste, and returning to the work station. For this analysis, differences in the type of copier are not particularly significant.

If the information entered on the form is being taken from another form or other printed material, be sure to add the reading time to the typing or handwriting elements. Then, if proofreading or verification is required, add that time factor as well.

The sorting and filing factors include taking a batch of 20 unsequenced documents, sorting them into the proper sequence, taking the sorted batch to the file cabinet(s), filing the documents into the front of the proper folder, and returning to the work station.

The factor for application of a gummed label is based on "licking" the label, as is usually done at a clerical work station. The factor would not apply to labels used in a shipping or mailing function where moistening brushes are available.

SPECIFICATIONS

If you go to an architect to have a house designed, one of the things the architect will do is develop a set of blueprints. The builder uses these prints to build your house. If the plans are followed correctly, your house should be exactly what you expect. If you ask for changes to the plans and do not check to see that the blueprints are actually altered, the chance for error greatly increases. Also, if the architect uses terms not familiar to the builder or includes unusual features that the builder is unaccustomed to, the chances for error are again increased.

Good blueprints make misunderstandings less frequent. (I know from experience that they don't eliminate all problems.) They also make it possible to speed up production, thereby reducing costs. A standard set of blueprints could be used to build many buildings, all identical.

A specification sheet for a form is like a blueprint for a house. It is the set of instructions that tells the forms manufacturerer how to build the form. It should contain all the construction details for the form. Be sure to put in writing any details discussed with the printer. That way any printer who gets the order will know exactly what you want.

Specifications should not be written in narrative style on the purchase order. A forms management function should have a well-designed specification sheet to help increase the productivity and effectiveness of its own paperwork needs. (If forms administrators don't have such a form, they really haven't earned the right to claim they can help others improve their paperwork.)

A form for a specification sheet appears in Chapter 7. That specification sheet is designed to be a master. It is filled out in pencil, for easy erasure for revisions. When a form is to be ordered, the specification sheet is photocopied as needed for that order. The original spec sheet is then refiled and used again and again for future orders. This reduces paperwork preparation time, cuts the chance of errors in transcription of information from one form to another, and assures greater accuracy and consistency in the information given to the manufacturer.

If your specification data is stored on a computer or a word-processing system that can produce multiple-part forms without clerical assistance or intervention, it is probably best to initiate a new specification sheet each time rather than copy a master. Few forms functions have this sort of on-line capability at this time; but, as electronics prices come down, more companies will be setting up such systems.

It is very critical to indicate on the spec sheet the date that the form is needed. Simply writing "As soon as possible" or "Rush" is not a good practice and can lead to serious misunderstandings with suppliers. (Normal delivery time for one manufacturer might be impossible for another.) It's best to indicate the actual date that you need the forms in your stock. If you need them tomorrow, say so. If you don't need them for 90 days, say that too. Be honest with your suppliers; it will encourage them to be honest with you.

6

Designing Forms
for Automation

MANY forms designers have told me about their reluctance to work on forms used with automated equipment. They've heard all the jargon: CRT, OCR, MICR, COM, MT/ST, remote terminal, distributed processing, time sharing, multi-programming, word processing, floppy disk, diskette, cassette, bits, bytes, bauds, facsimile, electronic mail, impact printing, non-impact printing, line printer, page printer, daisy-wheel printer, keypunch, keytape, paper tape, magnetic tape, bubble memory, and random access, just to name a few.

They've heard all these words and phrases, and are reluctant to get involved. They don't feel qualified to design forms for that equipment because they don't understand the equipment. In some cases, their fears have been promoted by consultants and suppliers who get paid to do jobs that they've convinced their customers are too complicated or confusing to be handled by laymen.

However, for a competent forms administrator, any fear of "computer" forms is completely unwarranted. In many ways an automated output form is the easiest kind to work on, and source documents (input forms) are not significantly different from non-computerized input forms. To help eliminate this fear of the unknown, we need to keep the computer in proper perspective. Once we understand what it does and how we get it to work for us, we can begin designing input and output forms.

To many people, a data processing system is a computer. Actually, computers and many other kinds of automated equipment are just parts of data processing systems. Included in the system are the people who provide the input data and those who receive, interpret, and act upon the output. A single person working with a piece of paper and a pencil constitutes a data processing system. We can extend the capabilities of that system by improving or adding to the equipment: substitute a ballpoint pen for the pencil; preprint a format on the paper; provide carbon paper or multiple-part forms; provide a calculator, a typewriter, a file cabinet, an automatic typewriter, a typewriter with magnetic storage, or a computer. Adding a computer to the system does not do anything magical or mysterious. Basically, the computer is a combination file, calculator, and typewriter, all controlled by a step-by-step procedure manual (program) that tells it exactly what to do. It will follow those programmed steps with extreme accuracy at an exceptional speed. Its potential output is greater than what hundreds or even thousands of people could do. But, it cannot do anything that people can't program it to do; it cannot think.

The computer is a very useful and valuable tool because of its ability to process information so rapidly and accurately. It enables us to get some kinds of information we could not get before because of the workhours needed for manual processing. The computer can help us do our jobs more productively and more effectively. However, it is possible that this ability to produce so much information can be misused. The computer can produce a lot of information that isn't needed. Mountain climbers may climb the mountain just because it is there. But in our business world, we really cannot afford that kind of thinking. We should not produce—using our computer or any other method—unnecessary information.

Sometimes systems analysts get so involved with maximum utilization of the computer that they neglect the people providing or using the information. Any computer system should be designed to serve the needs of the users, to make their jobs easier and more productive. People should never be required to sacrifice their productivity or effectiveness in order to use a computer more effectively. People should never be inconvenienced for the convenience of a machine.

HOW DOES A COMPUTER WORK?

Most of us have only a vague idea of how a computer actually works. We know that it operates on electricial impulses. All of its actions are based on the presence or absence of an electrical current. Our concern is not with the internal electronic processing—let's let the designers and engineers worry about those details. Our job is to help make sure that the alphabetic and numeric characters people read can be effectively converted to electrical impulses through whatever input device is used.

Early computers used tab cards, with punched holes, as the prime input media. Keypunch operators would read the source document and key in selected data on a typewriter-style keyboard, producing a card containing up to 80 characters. These cards were then input to the computer through a card reader unit. Tab cards are still used extensively today, but other alternatives are also available. The output of the input operator can be a magnetic tape or disk instead of cards. Or the keyboard may be hooked up directly to the computer. With OCR (optical character recognition) and MICR (magnetic ink character recognition) readers, it is also possible for the computer to accept typed, printed, and, in some cases, handprinted data right from the source document. These types of input forms are used for your personal checking account, remittance advices to return with your payments, credit card charge slips, and so on.

A look at a conventional tab card (Example 29) best illustrates the general concept of converting human-readable information to machine-readable data. This card consists of 80 vertical columns and

EXAMPLE 29

12 horizontal rows, allowing a total of 960 possible hole positions. A hole or combination of holes in one column represents one letter, number, or other character. Therefore, a conventional card contains a maximum of 80 characters.

As these cards are fed through the card reader, electrical impulses are allowed to pass through each hole punched in the card. By recognizing the location of each punch, the card reader "knows" which character and which card column to transmit to the computer. After the input data has been read in and processed, the electrical impulses have to be converted back to our language. To communicate with us, the computer normally prints on paper, using a high-speed printer. As forms designers, we are primarily and directly involved with this kind of output. Other output methods include the console typewriter, CRT screen display, punched cards, and even audible messages using combinations of prerecorded words and sounds.

Computers are not electronic brains. They can only follow the instructions given to them by a programmer. These instructions are very detailed, and include every single step of the required processing. Special programming languages have been developed to provide some shortcuts for the programmer. They combine many detailed steps into one inclusive command. COBOL, FORTRAN, and BASIC are among these languages.

Analysts and programmers start the programming process by reviewing the needs of the requester. They then develop both generalized and detailed flowcharts of the procedure. Using the detailed flowchart, each step is written in the programming language. The coded program is then punched or otherwise input to the computer, where it is converted, by another program, into machine language. After testing and any necessary corrections or revisions, the program is ready to use. (This process is quite similar to the process of analyzing and designing a form.)

Included in the program steps is a detailed description of each output record. Every data element must be identified, measured, and placed exactly on the output form. When designing a manually prepared form, we can get by, usually, with thinking "this will probably be about ten characters and take about one and a half or two inches." However, it's impossible for a programmer to make that type of calculation.

HOW DO WE DESIGN COMPUTER FORMS?

We design computer input and output forms (and those for other types of automation) using the same techniques that we use for non-computerized forms. We try to develop the best possible tool for everyone involved in the process. We have to guard against favoring one aspect of the total process at the expense of another.

Input Forms

On source documents (forms containing the data to be keyed into the computer) our job is to make the translation of data from the source document to the input medium as efficient and as accurate as possible, without detracting from other equally important, or even more important, uses of the form.

For example, a shipping order could be handwritten, sent to a warehouse for order filling, then sent to inventory control for posting to an inventory record with copies filed for reference during and after processing. Then, as a final step, the form may be sent for input to an invoicing program. We must resist the tendency to think of this form as a keypunch document that happens to include shipping information, rather than a shipping order that happens to be used for the computer input preparation.

Here are some techniques we can use to help the input operator:

Identify the input fields. Usually, only certain pieces of information are entered into the computer. The operator should not have to search for these items. Using shading and bold lines (Example 30) and separation are three methods for identifying the input fields.

Make the input information easy to read. Input operators are normally working at a fast pace. The data they use must be very legible. The space allowed must be adequate. If they do not receive the original document, the impression quality must be proper. The contrast between input data, captions, and background must be good, and the overall layout appropriate.

In this regard, designing an input form with a separate box for each character (a very common practice) is not advisable. Example 31 looks like a brick wall and, because of all the lines and the unnatural spacing of the characters, it is very difficult to read. Anyone using such a form is

EXAMPLE 30

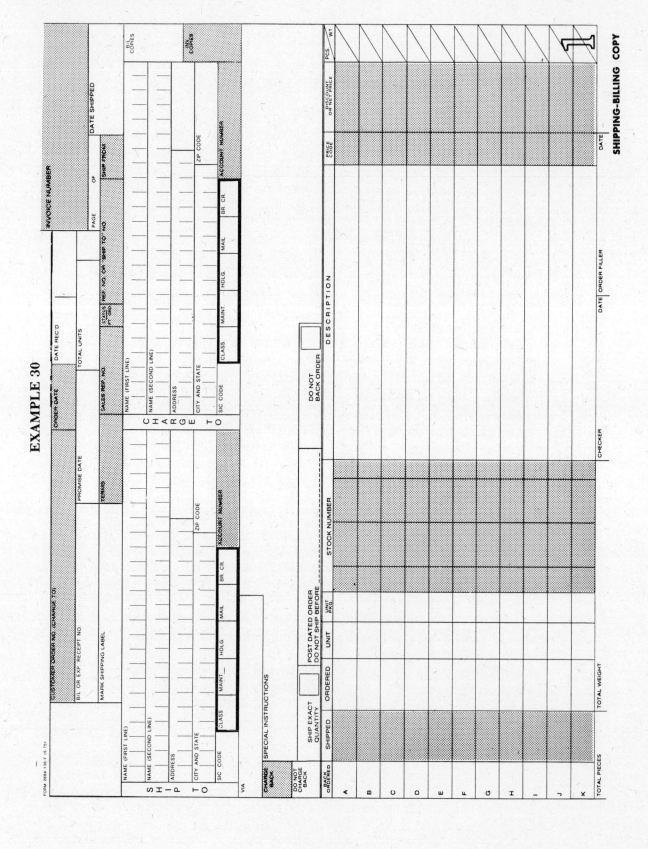

FORM 2884 136 F (5 75)

SHIPPING-BILLING COPY

EXAMPLE 31

FORM 7981-4

	1-10	11-20	21-30	31-40	41-50	51-60	61-70	71-80

EXAMPLE 32

DIS KEY PUNCH INPUT

FORM _____

SUBMITTED BY _____   PHONE _____   LOC _____   DATE _____   PAGE _____ OF _____

TERRITORY CODE			CK		CUSTOMER NUMBER						CK	UPDATE CODE																																											
1	2	3	4	5	6	7	8	9	10	11	12	13	14	15	16	17	18	19	20	21	22	23	24	25	26	27	28	29	30	31	32	33	34	35	36	37	38	39	40	41	42	43	44	45	46	47	48	49	50	51	52	53	54	55	56
1	2	3	4	5	6	7	8	9	10	11	12	13	14	15	16	17	18	19	20	21	22	23	24	25	26	27	28	29	30	31	32	33	34	35	36	37	38	39	40	41	42	43	44	45	46	47	48	49	50	51	52	53	54	55	56

bound to suffer eye fatigue after repeated attempts to read the fill-in data rapidly. This format leads the reader to look at each character individually rather than at a word, or even a phrase, at a time.

Screened lines, both horizontal and vertical, help soften the appearance of the form, reducing eyestrain and improving the readability of the entered information. This is true on all forms, but is especially applicable to source documents. A 20-percent screen is usually the most effective for this purpose. When screening a series of lines, it is advisable that every fourth or fifth line be solid. This helps anchor the reader's eyes, as shown in Example 32.

Make it easy to input the information in the correct spacing and sequence. The input sequence should be the same as the sequence on the form (which should be logically determined by preparation and usage factors). An input operator should not have to search from one spot on the form to another to find the next data field. We can also indicate card columns, field numbers, and maximum characters to help the operators.

In summary, use type styles and sizes, line weights, and screens to highlight, guide, or de-emphasize words, lines, or areas in order to help all users of the form, including the input operator.

The forms designer should work with the systems analysts and users in order to come up with the best arrangement on the input forms.

Magnetic Ink Character Recognition (MICR)

Banks use magnetic ink character recognition as a means of input for deposit/withdrawal accounting. (See Example 33.) MICR readers sense the significant shapes of the various numbers and characters, thereby bypassing any manual keying operations. In designing these forms, a designer must provide a specified area for the magnetic coding. This area, as well as other requirements, is shown on MICR layout sheets available from the forms manufacturer.

EXAMPLE 33

⑆0960⑈0112⑆ 0 10 10 23 24 7⑈06

CHECKS AND OTHER ITEMS ARE RECEIVED FOR DEPOSIT SUBJECT TO THE PROVISIONS OF THE UNIFORM COMMERCIAL CODE OR ANY APPLICABLE COLLECTION AGREEMENT

Optical Character Recognition (OCR)

I will not attempt to explain how these units function, other than that they "read" whatever is not reflected back to the scanning head. White paper reflects the light back. Black ink and other non-reflective inks do not, therefore they are read by the scanner, and their shape interpreted as a specific alphabetic or numeric character.

Generally, the preprinted format on the form is not to be read, therefore it must be printed in reflective ink. This makes it invisible to the scanner, just like the white paper.

Most machines require a timing mark, a unique character or line, that tells it where to start reading. This mark must be read; therefore, it must be printed in a readable ink (non-reflective).

Normally, the paper used would be OCR bond, with a weight of 20 to 26#, depending on the machine. This paper is specially made to minimize any impurities that would be "read" by the scanner, causing it to reject the record.

Output Forms

A computer output report may be a continuous form of various sizes and parts, or tab cards, either single or continuous. These output forms can be quite easy to design. Many of the problems we have to solve when designing a form do not exist if a computer is going to fill it out. Vertical and horizontal spacing allocation is determined by the computer printing unit and the programmer, fill-in instructions are not needed, the conditions of preparation are known and constant, the information to be preprinted and the fill-in data are both predetermined. In many cases, the entire print format is supplied by the programmer. An inexperienced forms designer can easily use the format supplied, other system parameters, and the printing unit capabilities to produce a good form layout for approval and composition. An experienced designer can take a more active role in determining the output format and providing it to the programmer.

Computer forms are easy to design because the preparation capabilities are constant. However, those same capabilities do not leave any margin for error. A handwritten form with line spacing of about 1/3″ might be satisfactory. Even a typed form with the same spacing would be usable, though definitely inefficient. Approximate spacing on a continuous output form simply will not work. If the width of a fill-in box is a little less than what is needed, a computer can't squeeze its "handwriting" to fit. All spacing must be exact.

Here are some suggestions to keep in mind when designing a continuous output form.

- Make a complete, exact-size layout, using layout paper that shows the computer printout spacing (lines per inch and characters per inch).
- Show an "X" in every possible print position for the output form in red pencil, to contrast with the black form layout.
- Indicate all perforations, marginal holes, and so on, so that users will be aware of the construction and appearance of the form.
- Remember to provide margins on all four sides of the form. It is best to leave at least ½″ on top and bottom and at least ³/₁₀″ on each side in addition to the marginal strip area.
- Provide at least a ⅝″ strip across the form for "lockup" on the press. This can be split between top and bottom, or it can be located anywhere on the form. If two or more colors are used, each color must have lockup space, which can be in the same or different location.
- Forms printed on a 6-line-per-inch printer must have a length that is evenly divisible by ⅙″. An 8-line-per-inch output requires a length divisible by ⅛″.
- Put vertical lines in the center of a print position with at least one blank space between entries. This minimum space is a necessity for the forms manufacturer. Allowing even more space between computer entries will make the form more legible.
- Perforations (vertical or horizontal) should also be in the center of a print position to allow for the normal tolerances in both manufacturing and computer printing.
- When designing a patterned carbon for selective imaging, manufacturing tolerances require an allowance equivalent to one print position at the edge of carbon areas.
- Use a minimum number of lines. They're not needed to guide the fill-in operation as they are on a handwritten or typed form. The only lines needed are those that will help the reader of the form.
- Check the requirements of your computer printer:
  Number of print positions per line (usually 132)
  Line spacing (usually 6 or 8 lines per inch)

> Form width limitations
> Impression capability
> Form thickness limitations

- Review the capabilities of your burster, decollator, and any other forms handling equipment.

Non-Impact Printing System

The latest computer printing systems developments are the non-impact printers, such as the IBM 3800 and the Xerox 9700. These systems combine computer and xerographic technologies in a unit that prints computer output data a page at a time. Their speed is very high compared with even the fastest line printer. We are concerned primarily with their effect on forms rather than with the technical aspects of how they work. From a forms standpoint, these units are significantly different from other printers.

- They print an entire page at one time rather than a line at a time
- They print only single-part forms
- The Xerox 9700 uses 8½″ × 11″ cut sheets, either blank or pre-printed
- They can be programmed to print the form layout and the output data simultaneously
- The IBM 3800 can also use a form slide for printing the layout
- They can print in various type styles and sizes—not just 10 characters per inch and 6 or 8 lines per inch
- When preprinted forms are used, certain inks are needed to withstand the heat used to set the image.

As with any other automated equipment, there are certain requirements for paper weights, sizes, and so on. The forms manuals provided by the equipment manufacturers will outline the exact needs of a specific printing system.

Even though programmers can now set up the complete layout for computer printing, forms designers should still be involved in the design phase. The only real difference is that the composition is done through programming rather than by a composer in the printshop.

Computer Output Microfilm (COM)

Another output possibility is "printing" directly on film, bypassing paper completely. COM units normally expose a form slide along with the output image so that the microform image looks like a printed form. Even though no paper is involved, forms designers should be responsible for layout of the form slide. Here again, you must review the specifications and requirements of the COM unit you have. Type sizes on COM slides should generally be equivalent to at least 8 points when projected.

Cathode Ray Tube Display (CRT)

With the advent of word-processing units and other types of remote terminals, a lot of information is being displayed on CRTs. Paper or film is not involved; however, the screen display is essentially a form. Good forms design techniques are just as important here as they are for paper forms. An experienced forms analyst and designer should be responsible for developing all CRT formats for both input and output operations.

Word Processors

These units use either cut sheets, like an ordinary typewriter, or continuous forms, like a computer. As with other automated output forms, specific requirements are found in the manufacturers' manuals.

7

Construction
of Forms

$\mathbf{F}$ORMS are basically sheets of paper with a printed format, so we will look first at paper characteristics, then at printing and binding methods, and finally at the various types of forms that can be constructed. As always, our objectives must be kept in mind. We are not trying to design the cheapest form nor the easiest one to produce. We should be constantly working to develop the best possible tools for the user.

PAPER

Selection of the proper paper is an important step in the design process. The types of paper normally used for forms are shown in Table 3. In general, most forms are printed on bond paper, which is available in many grades (see Table 4). Of these grades, the sulphite-4 is used most often.

The correct weight of paper for a particular form depends on the construction and usage of that form. For bond paper, use the following guide as a rule of thumb.

Single-sheet Forms		*Multiple-part Forms*	
Printed on one side	16#	First and last parts	15–16#
Printed on two sides	20#	Middle parts	11–12#

The weights shown above for multiple-part forms should provide legibility on forms of up to five parts, if filled out by hand or by a computer printer. If the form is prepared on an electric typewriter, the impression should remain legible through seven parts. If more parts are needed, test a "carbon dummy" on the equipment to be used. Manufacturers will provide this mock-up of the form for your testing.

Table 3. Types of paper and their uses in the construction of forms.

Type	Weight Range (pounds)	General Use
Manifold	4–10#	Carbon paper, sales receipts
Bond	12–28#	Most forms
Kraft	16–24#	Envelopes
Ledger	24–36#	Semipermanent records with frequent handling
Offset	40–70#	Labels, internally produced forms
Index	75–170#	Card forms, file folders
Tab card stock	99#	Tab cards for computer input forms
Safety	24#	Checks and negotiable documents

Table 4. Grades of bond paper.

Grade	Normal Lifetime	Usage
100% rag	100 years	Permanent
		Severe handling
75% rag	75 years	Severe handling
50% rag	50 years	Severe handling
25% rag	25 years	Much handling
100% sulphite-1	20 years	Normal handling
100% sulphite-2	15 years	Normal handling
100% sulphite-3	15 years	Normal handling
100% sulphite-4	15 years	Little handling
100% sulphite-5	15 years	Little handling

Carbon Paper

The carbon paper used in forms is "one-time" carbon, designed to be thrown away after a single use. The carbon coating transfers to the paper either from a gliding impression (handwriting) or from impact (typing or computer output). Usually, blue carbon is used for hand-prepared forms, and black carbon for those prepared by machine.

If selective imaging is desired, the carbon can be manufactured with coated and uncoated areas. Where there is no coating, no image is transferred. These patterned areas are much more effective than the cheaper alternative of hiding the information to be deleted by printing a blockout on the form itself. Blockouts do not look good on the form, and the information on the form is only partially hidden by the block-out pattern.

When the coated area is a continuous strip running parallel to the stub of the form, it is called strip carbon. This is the most economical type of partially-coated carbon paper. In cases where strip carbon is used, it might be possible to substitute a narrow piece of fully-coated paper. This would probably be even cheaper.

Patterns other than the strip running parallel to the stub require special plates and a separate printing operation that often must be done by another manufacturer. That type of patterned carbon is more expensive and requires a longer lead time for production.

Carbonless Paper

It is possible to produce multiple-part sets without carbon paper by using one of the several types of carbonless paper available.

Chemical carbonless is the most widely used type. Bond paper is coated using two chemicals—one on the back, the other on the front. When pressure is applied to these mated surfaces, an image is formed. The top sheet in a set needs the coating only on the back (CB). The last sheet is coated only on the front (CF). Intermediate parts are coated front and back (CFB). Many people call this product "NCR" paper, meaning "no carbon required." This is a misuse of the trademark of Appleton Papers, Inc., which is used to identify many of its products—including its brand of carbonless paper.

Self-contained carbonless includes both of the chemicals needed to produce an image on or in the same sheet. It can be used for various ribbonless entries as well as for ordinary set constructions.

Mechanical transfer paper has a colored coating, usually gray, on the back of the sheet. Pressure on the sheet causes the coating to transfer to the front of the next sheet, an action very similar to carbon paper.

We have experienced good legibility with up to five parts of the chemical carbonless paper on widely used handwritten or typed forms, and up to six parts on computer output forms. In other applications, where the preparation is limited to fewer people, seven-part handwritten forms are used successfully and an eleven-part form is typed satisfactorily.

Generally, it appears that a multiple-part carbonless set will produce an image comparable with a carbon set of the same number of parts, unless premium papers and carbons are used.

Carbonless sets are easier to use than those with carbon. You don't have to look for a place to dispose of the carbon. You don't have to wash up after handling a few sets. More sets are stored in the same amount of space. Freight charges are lower. More forms per carton means less computer downtime to change cartons. In-plant production capability means low-usage forms can be produced economically in unit sets as needed.

It is possible to combine carbonless paper and carbon paper in the same set. For example, if a form has to be written on both sides, construct it to write on the carbon-interleaved side first. Then, remove the carbon, turn the form over, and write on the carbonless side. Or, the first several parts may be carbonless for convenience and the latter plies may be carbon-interleaved for economy and legibility.

New developments now allow the forms manufacturer to sensitize selected areas of any part right on the press, providing selective imaging capabilities as with a patterned carbon.

At this time, carbonless sets usually cost a little more. But, in my opinion, the benefits of using them far outweigh the cost differential.

PRINTING AND BINDING

Most forms are printed on rotary presses. The plate is wrapped around a cylinder which turns as the paper is transported through the press. The paper is either fed through in sheets (sheet-fed) or in a roll (web). Rolls may be either rolled up again after printing (web-to-web), or cut to sheets at the end of the press (web-to-sheet). Presses may have multiple cylinders for printing multiple colors on the same run, and some can even handle several rolls of paper as well.

The circumference of the cylinder determines the form sizes that can be produced on that press. Common press sizes and their related form sizes are shown here.

Cylinder	Form Depth (stub dimension)
8½″	2⅚, 4¼, 8½
11″	3⅔, 5½, 11
14″	3½, 7, 14
17″	2⅚, 4¼, 5⅔, 8½
22″	3⅔, 5½, 7⅓, 11
24″	3, 4, 6, 8, 12

After printing, various other things can be done to help make the form a better tool. Holes can be punched or drilled as needed for binders. Preforating can be done to help separate sheets, as for a tear-off label. The form can be scored (creased) to aid in folding, especially with card stock. Holes, slots, windows, and so on can be die-cut as specified. Padding, collating, numbering, and packaging are also bindery operations.

TYPES OF CONSTRUCTION

Single-Sheet Construction

General description. As the name implies, these forms are simply a single sheet of paper.

Printing method. Single sheets can be produced on any kind of printing, duplicating, or copying equipment. They may be numbered, perforated, die-cut, punched, and so on after printing.

Standard sizes. The most widely used size is 8½″ × 11″. However, the paper comes in sheets of 34″ × 22″ (bond or offset), and any size that can be cut from that sheet without waste is a standard size, assuming it can be printed on the available equipment.

The normal standard sizes are 17″ × 11″, 8½″ × 11″, 8½″ × 7⅓″, 8½″ × 5½″, and 4¼″ × 5½″.

Card stock standards are different, with 3″ × 5″, 4″ × 6″, 8″ × 5″, and 8″ × 10″ being the normal sizes.

While there are definite advantages to using a standard size both in the production and usage, a single-sheet form can and should be cut to special sizes whenever so doing will improve the productivity and effectiveness of the form users.

Normal applications. Single sheets are practical and advisable when only one part is needed, when the quantities used are quite small, and when they are not inventoried by a supply function.

Padded Sheets

General description. Basically, padded sheets are single sheets that are bound together on one edge with a padding compound.

Printing method. Same as for single sheets.

Standard sizes. Standard sizes are the same as single sheets. Most bindery operators will pad about 100 sheets to a pad unless otherwise specified. The correct pad size should be based on average usage by an individual. As an example, if each user needs about 25 forms per year, the pads should consist of about 25 sheets rather than 100.

Normal applications. Pads are convenient when single parts are used and the forms are stocked by a supply group, but large quantities are kept on hand by the users. Padded sheets store better and make order filling and inventory control much more effective. It is much easier to fill an order for two pads than to count out 200 sheets.

Unit Sets

General description. Two or more sheets, held together by a glued stub or a padded edge; made of carbonless paper or carbon-interleaved paper.

Printing method. Could be printed on either a sheet-fed press or a web press. Relatively small quantities of carbonless sets would usually be prepared using pre-collated sets of paper on a sheet press. A special padding compound is then used to produce these carbonless sets.

Larger quantities of carbonless sets and carbon-interleaved sets are produced more economically on the faster web-to-web presses. Each part is printed separately and these rolls are then collated and glued, after which the glued sets are cut apart on a collator.

Both of the above methods generally use offset plates. It is also possible to use a raised-surface plate on an impact printing press and print all parts of a carbonless set at one time. This is, of course, more economical because of the reduction in press time.

Standard sizes. For sets produced on a sheet-fed press, the same standard sizes apply as for single sheets and pads.

On web presses, the size of the printing cylinder must be considered when selecting sizes. The dimension perpendicular to the stub can be any reasonable size, and is normally such that the form size is comparable to a standard cut sheet size applicable to the user's needs. The stub size, usually ½″, ⅝″, or ¾″, must be added to the desired sheet size to express the actual form size. For example, if an 8½″ × 11″ sheet is needed after the parts are separated, the overall size with the stub would be either 9¼″ × 11″ or 8½″ × 11¾″, depending on the location of the stub.

Normal applications. Whenever more than one part is needed, a unit set provides a ready-to-use form with no registration problems, no make-ready work, little cleanup afterward (none if carbonless paper is used), and no lost time or effort making copies.

Design tips.
- On typed forms, the stub should be on the top if possible.
- On handwritten forms, the stub is best on the left side.
  These two tips assure that any pulling pressure on the form during preparation is at right angles to the stub. Pulling at other angles will cause poor registration on most of the parts other than the original.
- If one part is to be removed prior to the others, make that part about ¼″ longer for easy recognition and removal.
- On carbon-interleaved sets, the carbons should be about ½″ shorter than the paper to provide a space for gripping or pulling only the paper when separating the set.
- Colored papers add quick visual recognition of parts for relatively little additional cost, as long as the manufacturer's normal colors and, in some cases, the standard sequence are used.

Books

General description. For our purposes, books are described as a number of unit sets held together by a stapled stub, with a cover for protection and rigidity.

Printing method. Same as for unit sets. After the sets are printed and collated, covers and chipboard are added and the entire package is stapled, or possibly padded. The covers are usually printed on a sheet-fed press because, in general, only relatively small quantities are needed.

Standard sizes. Same as for unit sets, except that books might have a double stub.

Normal applications. Used to provide an easy, convenient, and neat way to carry a number of unit sets. Particularly suited for use by sales clerks, sales representatives, or others who do not work at a desk or other type of administrative work station.

Design tips.

- A glued stub at the end opposite the stapled stub makes it easier to remove the set or to insert the cover flap under the top set to prevent "write-through" (when writing shows up on more than one set).
- Instructions printed on the inside of the cover are available to the user as the form is being filled out.
- If necessary for control purposes, one part may be left in the book by simply omitting the perforation at the stapled stub. This should not be done unless absolutely necessary as the sheets left in the book make usage of the remaining forms more difficult.

Continuous *

General description. These are single-part or multiple-part forms produced from a roll. They are not cut apart prior to use, but are perforated between sets for mechanical or manual separation, if desired.

Printing method. Must be printed on a web-to-web press. Normally collated and interleaved with carbon paper (if carbonless paper is not used) and then folded on a collator.

* See also Chapter 6, "Designing Forms for Automation."

Normal standard sizes. The form depths listed earlier in this section apply to continuous forms. A further consideration is that the depth of the form must be evenly divisible by ⅙″ or ⅛″ (computer output line spacing), unless special programming techniques are used.

Normal applications. Used on computer printers, word-processing output units, automatic typewriters, and so on.

Envelopes

General description. Envelopes are designed to contain something else, usually another form. May have a die-cut window allowing the name and address on the internal document to show through.

Printing method. Printed on either sheets or rolls and then die-cut, folded, and glued to form the envelope.

Standard sizes. Sizes are highly standardized due to the construction method and mailing requirements. Standard sizes and types of envelopes are shown in Table 5. Envelope manufacturers will usually supply you with templates and samples of the various sizes available. The standard window size is 1⅛″ × 4½″. It is located ½″ from the bottom of the envelope and ⅞″ from the left edge.

Sizes other than those shown in Table 5 are available, but care must be taken to assure their acceptability for mailing and the possibility of a postage surcharge for certain sizes. Current regulations require that any mailing piece must be at least 3½″ high, 5″ wide, and .007″ thick. If any dimension of card or envelope is less than one of these minimums, it is not mailable. First class or single-piece third class mail is subject to extra postage if any dimension exceeds 6⅛″ high, 11½″ wide, or ¼″ thick, or if the width of the envelope is not between 1.3 and 2.5 times the height. (See Example 34.)

Table 5. Standard sizes of envelopes.

Type	Number	Size (inches)
Commercial sizes	6¼	3½ × 6
	6¾	3⅝ × 6½
	7	3¾ × 6¾
	7¾ (Monarch)	3⅞ × 7½
	8⅝ (Check)	3⅝ × 8⅝
	9	3⅞ × 8⅞
	10	4⅛ × 9½
	11	4½ × 10⅜
	12	4¾ × 11
	14	5 × 11½
Booklet sizes	2½	4½ × 5⅞
	3	4¾ × 6½
	5	5½ × 8⅛
	6	5¾ × 8⅞
	6½	6 × 9
	7	6¼ × 9⅝
	7½	7½ × 10½
	9	8¾ × 11½
	9½	9 × 12
	10	9½ × 12⅝
Open-end sizes	1 coin	2¼ × 3½
	3 coin	2½ × 4¼
	4 coin	3 × 4½
	4½ coin	3 × 4⅞
	5 coin	2⅞ × 5¼
	5½ coin	3⅛ × 5½
	6 coin	3⅜ × 6
	7 coin	3½ × 6½
	Unnumbered	5½ × 8¼
		6 × 9
		6½ × 9½
		7 × 10
		7½ × 10½
		9 × 12
		9½ × 12½
		10 × 13
		11½ × 14½

EXAMPLE 34

Standard maximum height — — — — — — — — — to 11.5" ▶

Corner of envelope must fall within these two lines to qualify as a standard shape.

5"

Minimum dimensions

3¹/₂

to 11.5" ▶

8

Necessary Tools
and Facilities

THE forms administration department should be the leading proponent and example of effective paperwork in the organization. There is no excuse for poor forms in a forms function. This chapter describes, illustrates, and applies the principles and procedures outlined in previous chapters.

We will look at the tools and facilities required to implement an effective forms administration program. They fall into three catagories: physical facilities, reference tools, and well-designed forms.

A forms group must be especially concerned about its own product. This chapter includes a description of the types of forms needed and a layout of each one. You may need to add only your company's identification and an appropriate code number to make them suitable for your own use. Or the layouts may serve as the starting point for your own design.

PHYSICAL FACILITIES

The physical facilities provided will significantly affect the performance of any group. The area must be comfortable, attractive, and appropriate for the work to be done. A forms group should be located in an area accessible to the many "customers" and supplier representa-

117

tives who will be visiting. In most cases, the user or requester of a form will want to discuss the needed form. A good location will help to encourage productive contacts.

Forms analysts and designers should each have their own private office—or at least a separate work area—where they can meet with forms requesters or supplier representatives. Privacy is important so that attention is not lost, train of thought is not broken, and confidential information is not overheard. When not discussing forms with someone, the analyst will need to concentrate on analyzing the information and preparing the layout of a form. An open office area will not allow the complete concentration that is necessary.

The analyst will need a desk or table with a large work surface on it. It should have kneespace on at least two sides so that two people can work together comfortably while looking at forms layouts and so on. The analyst will also need a bookcase or credenza to store samples of forms, papers, and type styles, copies of magazine articles, and files of work in process. These materials have to be close at hand and well organized. Some analysts like to do their layout work on a drafting table, but this is not generally necessary. The additional equipment can take up too much space in the office area. A normal desk top is usually suitable for doing layout work.

Each analyst should have a separate telephone. No one should have to wait for someone else to get off the phone.

A nearby copy machine is a necessity. Analysts will not need to make many copies of an original, but they will often need a few copies of their pencil layouts or existing forms. Spacing on forms is critical, so photocopies must be exactly the same size as the original. An enlargement or reduction of only 1 or 2 percent will make the copy unacceptable.

For drawing the layouts, a good, fine-point pencil is essential. (I prefer one of the .5 mm mechanical pencils.) A good eraser is also needed. (Forms designers seldom make mistakes, but they do change their minds a lot.) A forms-designer ruler, which has four scales (1/4″, 1/6″, 1/10″, and mm), complete the necessary tools. Other helpful items are scissors, a knife, transparent tape that can be written on, double-faced tape, red and blue pencils, opaque fluid, and a simple pocket calculator.

Good, glare-free lighting is important. The light in most modern offices is usually adequate—nothing special is required.

NUMBERING SYSTEMS

A numbering system is probably the most basic reference tool used by a forms administration department. There are many numbering systems in use; in fact, there's probably a different one for every forms group in the country. Some are very simple, others quite complex. Some are nonsignificant (the numbers themselves do not mean anything), some are significant (the various parts of the number are reference codes telling something about the form), and others are a combination of both.

Some departments may already be using an existing numbering system. If that system works, it is best not to change it when the forms administration program is established. Changing all the numbers, which would probably mean revising manuals, instruction sheets, and, of course, the forms themselves, involves a lot of work and could cause a great deal of confusion. However, if the system in use is complex and unwieldy, revising it may be beneficial in the long run.

In setting up a new numbering system, first consider how the number will be used. The most prevalent use of the form number is to identify the form when:

Ordering from the supplier
Ordering from office supply stock
Maintaining inventory records
Referring to the form in procedures
Filing the form

The form number must be copied from one document to another, found in a list, file, or other type of recording system, or read and recognized in written material. This suggests that the best number has only a few digits, a simple structure, and is easy to remember, say, and write.

In the simplest numbering system, forms are numbered consecutively starting with 1. No significance is built into such a system. In most organizations, a form number would never exceed four digits. It would be rare for any size organization using this system to have form numbers that exceed five digits. This meets the requirements of being short and simple.

The above system can be varied slightly by the addition of an alphabetic or numeric prefix to the number to code for a particular department. For example, PR123 might be a payroll form, and AR123 an accounts receivable form. Each department would have a prefix and its own series of numbers beginning with 1. The prefixes can be alphabetic abbreviations of the functions represented, for example, PR for payroll, AR for accounts receivable, FA for forms administration, EN for engineering, PE for personnel, PU for purchasing, and so on. They could also be numeric codes, such as the accounting codes for the particular functions.

The code can be made more elaborate by expanding the number of digits. For example, PR-1-223 might be a payroll check and AP-1-228 an accounts payable check, with the 1 following the alphabetic prefix signifying a check. Or PR123, PR123-1, and PR123-2 might be three similar or related forms (such as a time card, payroll check, and a payroll register) used in the same system. Information about the construction, number of parts, size, supplier, and even designer of a form can be coded into the number.

Some companies combine the form numbering system with a cross-reference system. This is possible, and not unusual, but makes updating the cross-reference system impractical—all the form numbers must be changed. When changing the system or the codes is too impractical, it usually goes undone and results in outdated information.

When a form is revised, that information should be coded into the form number. This will facilitate production of the right form, proper inventory control, and proper filing and referencing. Most companies show the month and year of the revision in parentheses after the number: PR123 (11/77). However, it is simpler to use a single letter suffix, which is easier to remember, recognize, and record. If the 11/77 version of a form was the second revision, the number would appear as PR123-B. People using or ordering the form would not know the revision date, but they don't really need that information. The file on that form will contain the ordering history, including dates, and other information that does not need to be coded into the form number.

Another suffix can be used to indicate that the form is not stocked. One company uses the abbreviation PWO (print when ordered) to show this. If form PR123-B were not stocked, the number would be PR123-B-PWO.

When a form becomes obsolete, the form number should be retired along with the file. Reusing numbers can lead to confusion. And if the number is not reissued on another form, it may be reinstated on the same form if it becomes an active form once more. This is not an unusual situation.

Maintaining Files

Every business function needs a memory—a selective, organized collection of data—to help make future decisions. In a forms administration department, the basic memory system is a file folder for each form, filed by form number. This folder should contain:

The original request for the form
Analysis worksheets
Specifications, past and present
Form samples, past and present
Reprint notices and obsolete notices
Purchase order or requisition copies
Any pertinent correspondence

Files on forms in use will be growing and active ones. Every person in the department should have convenient, rapid access to them. Folders with side tabs stored on open shelves are ideal for this kind of filing system.

The folders should always be in their normal place in the file unless some action is being taken. For example, while waiting for a piece of information, a folder should be refiled, not held in a desk drawer. The information should always be available for use by someone else, and is too valuable to be misplaced.

CROSS-REFERENCE SYSTEMS

A good cross-reference system is needed to identify:

- All forms used by one department or other portion of the organization
- Forms that perform the same function (all checks, production reports, call reports, invoices, purchase orders, and so on)
- Forms with similar construction (pads, unit sets, continuous forms, and so on)
- Forms of the same size, same number of parts, and so on

121

The cross-reference system should be able to identify a variety of characteristics in combination, for example, all unit-set call reports used by the sales department, 8½″ × 11″, with three parts of carbonless paper. The information is then used to:

Analyze possibilities for combining several forms
See if a minor revision on an existing form will satisfy a new need
Review the complete paperwork process of a department or division
Combine orders for better pricing by outside suppliers
Provide information to answer inquiries

Types of Systems

Cross-reference systems vary from simple handwritten lists to folders with forms samples, from periodic computer listings to work-processing or computerized on-line systems. No matter which system is used, the reference codes should be designed so that the organization will get maximum benefit. A system that is hard to use or difficult to keep up to date will be ignored, and all the effort to establish it will be wasted.

Lists

A small company can probably use, very effectively, a handwritten list as its cross-reference system. This list would be broken down by department or other organizational designation. For example, forms may be filed under the following:

Payroll	Inventory	General accounting
Accounts payable	Cashier	Cost accounting
Accounts receivable	Purchasing	Data processing
Credit	Receiving	Marketing
Sales	Shipping	Administration
Production	Warehousing	General use

This type of cross-reference list would include all forms originated by each department, regardless of the function of the form. The number of forms on each list would probably be quite small, so having checks, time cards, and registers all on the payroll list, for example, would not be a handicap. However, an analyst who wanted to find all forms with the same function would have to search all appropriate lists; the forms would not appear together in one place.

With this kind of system, it is best to keep sample forms in the file maintained for each form. That way, the most recent sample will always be available for review. If sample forms are filed together by function, maintaining the latest samples in those functional folders is a very tedious, time-consuming task. In fact, those folders are rarely kept up to date.

Multiple-Part Card Files

Handwritten lists are usually too cumbersome for larger organizations; they can use multiple-part forms. The codes are indicated on 3″ × 5″ index cards, which are filed in the appropriate sections of the cross-reference index file.

Edge-Punched Card File

Another method is to use edge-punched cards, those with either round holes (Keysort) or notches in the bottom, for mechanical or magnetic selection. All forms with the desired characteristics can be located at one time by selecting the proper code. These systems are very practical for up to about 4,000 forms.

Tab Listings

If keypunch, sorting, and listing equipment is available, a single tab card can be punched for each form, including all of the various reference information. These cards can then be sorted and listed in various sequences. This is very similar to a computerized listing, but does not actually involve any computer processing.

On-Line Computer File

More advanced systems use the same basic coding structure. These are incorporated into some sort of magnetic storage, either an on-line computer terminal or a word-processing unit with storage capabilities that can accommodate the organization's cross-reference file.

A versatile on-line system might be useful for one group but ridiculously impractical for another. The important thing is to establish some way to locate a form or a group of forms by any one of several identifiers.

Sample Cross-Reference System

The following cross-reference system is currently in use at one large company.

A tab card is prepared for each form, and these cards are periodically sorted and listed by each of the reference codes discussed below. The information punched in each card includes:

Form number	10 positions
Form title	36 positions
Originating department	4 positions
Operation performed (function)	2 positions
Company organizational area	3 positions
Type of form (construction)	2 positions
Size of the form	2 positions
Number of parts in the form	2 positions

The *form number, title,* and *number of parts* are not coded. The actual information is used. The *originating department* is indicated by the regular four-digit department number used for that department throughout the accounting system.

The *operation code* is a two-digit alphabetic abbreviation of the operation or function of the form. In many cases, it comes close to being the title of the form, or a word from the title. Following is the list of codes that are applicable to this company.

AK	Acknowledgment	EN	Envelope
AJ	Adjustment (complaint)	ES	Estimate
AG	Agreement (contract)	EX	Explanation
AP	Application	FO	Folder
AU	Authorization	FR	Forecast
BI	Bid	ID	Identification
BL	Bill of lading	IF	Inform
CR	Call Report	IS	Instruction
CA	Cancellation	IR	Inventory report
CE	Certification	IN	Invoice
CH	Check	LA	Label
CI	Computer input	LY	Layout
CM	Credit memo	LT	Load ticket
DM	Debit memo	NO	Notification
DO	Desk order	PY	Pay
DF	Draft	PA	Performance appraisal

PI	Personnel information	RE	Request
PD	Production order	RQ	Requisition
PR	Production report	RV	Revision, change
PS	Production schedule	SO	Sales order
PO	Purchase order	SC	Schedule
QO	Quotation	SH	Shipping order
RR	Receiving report	SS	Shipping schedule
RC	Recording (misc.)	ST	Statement
RL	Record payroll information	TA	Tag
RG	Registration	TR	Test report
RJ	Reject	WS	Work Schedule
RP	Reporting (misc.)	WT	Worksheet

The *company organizational area*, which in some cases identifies the same department as the originating department number, is a three-digit alphabetic code set up to identify three levels of the organization. The first digit shows the major area of the company, such as finance, or one of the several major sales groups; the second digit breaks out a portion of the group, such as the payroll function within finance. The last digit identifies the functional area within the group, division, or department, such as sales, marketing, engineering, production, data processing, accounting, laboratory, and so on.

As you can see from reviewing this list, coding is not an exact science. It is sometimes difficult to know just how to identify or locate a particular form. If one person does all of the coding, the system will usually become internally consistent. This can be very valuable when looking for a form or forms in any cross-reference system.

The form's construction is identified by a two-digit numeric code. The codes and construction used in this system are given here.

01	Pad	12	Postcard
02	Unit set	13	Tag
03	Single sheet	14	Envelope
04	Continuous	15	Window envelope
05	Book or manual	16	Gummed label
06	Salesbook or orderbook	17	Pressure-sensitive label
07	Tab card	18	Stencil label
08	Microfilm aperture card	19	Carbonized label
09	"Kardex" card	20	File folder
10	"Wheeldex" card	21	Mailer
11	"Visirecord" card	22	Continuous self-mailer
		30	Other

125

The form's size is coded by an alphabetic character, as shown below. (The sizes shown here are given in inches.) An asterisk may be placed in front of the code if the size is close to but not exactly the one listed.

A	3×5	N	$8\frac{1}{2} \times 11\frac{3}{4}$	
B	$3\frac{1}{4} \times 5\frac{1}{2}$ (postcard)	O	$9\frac{1}{4} \times 11$	
C	$3\frac{1}{4} \times 6\frac{1}{2}$	P	$9\frac{7}{8} \times 11$	
D	$3\frac{1}{4} \times 7\frac{3}{8}$ (tab card)	Q	11×17	
E	$3\frac{2}{3} \times 8\frac{1}{2}$	R	$14\frac{7}{8} \times 11$	
F	4×6	S	$6\frac{1}{2} \times 3\frac{5}{8}$ (#6 envelope)	
G	$4\frac{1}{4} \times 5\frac{1}{2}$	T	$8\frac{7}{8} \times 3\frac{3}{8}$ (#9 envelope)	
H	$5\frac{1}{2} \times 6\frac{1}{2}$ (double postcard)	U	$9\frac{1}{2} \times 4\frac{1}{8}$ (#10 envelope)	
I	$5\frac{1}{2} \times 8\frac{1}{2}$	V	$6\frac{1}{2} \times 9\frac{1}{2}$ (envelope)	
J	$5\frac{1}{2} \times 9\frac{1}{4}$	W	$9\frac{1}{2} \times 12$ (envelope)	
K	$6\frac{1}{4} \times 8\frac{1}{2}$	X	$4\frac{1}{2} \times 11^{5}/_{16}$ (envelope)	
L	7×8	Y	Envelope, misc.	
M	$8\frac{1}{2} \times 11$	Z		

The information needed for coding and punching cross-reference data is maintained on a form number register like the one shown later in this chapter (see "Well-Designed Forms").

ORDER-STATUS MONITORING SYSTEM

A system that allows rapid reference to the status of any order in process is also a necessity for an effective forms administration program. A large forms group may process 1,000 or more orders each month for printing or buying forms. It is obvious that each of these orders cannot be followed up on an individual basis. A good system eliminates the need for continual routine follow-up by highlighting problem areas. Most orders can be processed, printed, and received without any intervention or follow-up by forms personnel. If this is not true in a particular organization, there is something wrong with the system.

Even in the best system, however, some orders have to be expedited. A few will be misplaced and will have to be found. Some will have to be modified. Some will be canceled. The forms group must maintain records that will help find any order at any time. However, this type of recording should not be a time-consuming process. It's nonproductive if much time is taken to record data that is needed in just a few instances.

The first place to look when checking up on an order is in the form's file. It should include a copy of the purchase requisition or in-plant job ticket and a copy of the specifications. This indicates that an order has been placed, and spells out exactly what was ordered.

The order registers shown in the next section provide further information on the order status, and a means of follow-up on exceptional items.

Like all reference tools, these systems must be maintained or they will be useless. A folder filed in the wrong place can cause hours of wasted time. (It seems that as soon as a folder is misfiled, an immediate, urgent need for it develops.) A cross-reference system that is accurate only 80 percent of the time is not much better than no system at all. An order-control system that does not accurately show the status of every order cannot be used to identify the exceptional ones. Keeping each of these tools up to date must become part of the group's normal routine; it must be built into the department's operating system.

WELL-DESIGNED FORMS

The forms included in this section provide the information needed by an effective forms group. Specific information needs may vary from one organization to another and desires for information will vary from one analyst to another. These forms probably cannot be used exactly as is by any group; hopefully, they will be a starting point for designing effective forms for your use. If they do fit your situation, and you want to use them as they are, perhaps with the addition of your company identification and a form number, feel free to do so.

The forms illustrated (shown here reduced) and explained are

Form Request
Form Number Register
Form Reprint Notice
Inactive Form Notice
Print When Ordered (PWO) File Update
Outside Purchase Order Register
Reproduction Job Number Register
Form Specifications
Form Specifications—Reproduction
Monthly Activity Report
Layout Sheets

Form Request

Purpose

The form request is used to gather and record some of the information needed to analyze, design, and order a form. It can also be used as a control document to see that all requests for new or revised forms have been properly approved by the appropriate department heads.

Construction

This is a two-part carbonless form, 8½″ × 8½″. The requester keeps one part as a record of the request and the forms group keeps the original to use in processing the request. Note on the form provided that a copy of the specification sheet is sent to the requester as confirmation of the order for a new form. If this is not done, the request should probably be a three-part form—the third part is returned to the requester as confirmation of the order.

Usage

As you can see by looking at the form, the requester is first asked to justify the need for a new form—why a new document should be created.

The requester is also asked to explain the distribution, filing, retention, and disposition of each copy of the form. This helps the person think through the entire system to make sure it is the best that can be developed. If users are not asked for this kind of information, forms are often requested before procedures have been thoroughly planned or reviewed. The forms analyst uses the information to determine the proper construction (number of parts and so on) of the new form.

The analyst needs information on how the form is to be filled out and the quantities to be used ("preparation") to properly design and order the form.

If they are known, specifications for the form may be filled in in the last section. However, the forms group does have the final responsibility for this portion of the process. The lower right corner provides space for the mailing address for single-user forms, a charge code (if needed), and the requester's name, department number, and so on. It also includes a spot for approval by a department head. Depending on the management attitudes of the organization, approval may or may not be necessary.

Form
Request

FORM

Send white copy of the Request and suggested layout to: FORMS ADMINISTRATION
Keep canary copy for your record. On new forms, you will receive a copy of the specification sheet as confirmation.

		Form Number
Form Title		

Reason *Describe reason for new form or revision, include any savings or other benefits*		☐ New ☐ Revision ☐ Permanent ☐ Temporary

Usage *Describe purpose, distribution, filing, retention, and disposition of each copy of form*	

Preparation
Indicate how the form will be filled out and the quantities to be used

SOURCE	☐ Multiple locations	☐ Single location *(specify)* (See Mailing Address below)	
PERSONNEL	☐ Clerical	☐ Production	☐ Other *(specify)*
METHOD	☐ Handwriting	☐ Typewriter	☐ Other *(specify)*
VOLUME USED	Quantity	Units ☐ Ea. ☐ Pads ☐ Bks.	Period ☐ Wk. ☐ Mon. ☐ Yr.

Suggested Specifications
Fill in if known.
Attach drawing of form, showing any additional specifications.
Forms Administration will write the final specs.

ORDER QUANTITY	Quantity	Units	Mailing Address		
SIZE	Width ,,	Height ,,			
NO. PARTS		☐ All White ☐ Colors	Charge Code (for non-stock forms)		Date Needed
PAPER	☐ Bond ☐ Carbonless	☐ Other	Requested by		Date
CONSTRUCTION	☐ Sheets ☐ Sets	☐ Pads ☐ Books	Department Name		Dept. No.
	☐ Continuous		Address		Phone
PRE-NUMBERING	☐ Yes, start with: ☐ No		Approved by (Dept. Head) ▶		Date

Form Number Register

Purpose

This register is used by the forms group to record the form numbers assigned to new forms, as well as the title and other necessary information about that form. It also includes data for the cross-reference system.

Construction

This is a single-sheet form printed on either a ledger sheet or 70# offset paper, 11″ × 8½″. It should be hole-punched to fit in a three-ring binder.

Usage

Whenever a number is assigned to a new form, the designer records the information requested in all columns from left to right through "Dept." If form numbers are assigned in a simple chronological sequence, the appropriate number for a new form will always be indicated by looking at the last number assigned. The last six columns on the register should be filled in periodically. If this is done by the same person, the code used will be internally consistent for cross-reference purposes.

FORM NUMBER REGISTER

FORM

FORM NUMBER	PWO	FORM TITLE	REQUESTER	DATE REQUESTED	DEPT.	OP	PROD. DIV.	TYPE	PROD	SIZE	PLIES

Form Reprint Notice

Purpose

The reprint notice is used to notify the requester of the form that the balance on hand has reached a reorder point. This gives the requester an opportunity to indicate whether a revision is needed and whether usage quantities will vary during the next 12 months, or to provide any other appropriate information.

Construction

This is a carbonless, two-part unit set, 8½″ × 8½″. The original is sent to the requester; the copy is maintained as a control over reprints in process and as a come-out for automatic reordering. The form reprint notice can be sent through interoffice mail systems without an envelope by simply folding and stapling the sheet with either the top address or the lower preprinted address showing.

Usage

After receiving notice from the office supply department that the form has reached a reorder point, the forms group enters the requester's name and address on the form, along with the form title, number, and the current date. The name of the analyst is entered in the lower left area. You will note that quantities on hand or to be ordered are not shown on the form, as this information is needed only by the forms group. The requester should be concerned about how many forms are expected to be used in the next year—not about how many to order.

The second part of the reprint notice is retained in a come-out file by date. As the originals are returned by the requester with the requested information, the control copy is pulled from the date file and destroyed. The original is then used to find the form's folder. Then the reordering process is started. If the original is not returned by the requester within ten days, as indicated on the form, the control copies are pulled and used to start the reorder process as if they were the originals returned by the requesters.

FORM REPRINT NOTICE

To
Dept. - Bldg. - Flr.

FORM

Form Title	Form No.	Date of Notice

The inventory of this form has reached the reorder point.

In order to insure a continuous supply, our reorder (either reprint or revision) must be placed within 2 weeks of the above date.

IF WE DO NOT RECEIVE THIS NOTICE WITHIN 2 WEEKS OF THE ABOVE DATE, THE FORM WILL BE REPRINTED "AS IS" BASED UPON PAST USAGE.

If you are no longer responsible for this form, return the notice immediately, with the name and address of the responsible person below:

Notice should be sent to ⟶

Please think about this form, and all your forms.

Let's work together to find a better way.

We will be glad to discuss with you both forms control and paperwork simplification methods that you can use to improve your paperwork.

Thank you in advance for your cooperation in making sure that your function has all of the forms it <u>needs</u>, and none that it does <u>not need</u>.

If you have any questions, Please Contact ▶

— Please complete this section —

DESIGN AND CONSTRUCTION

☐ OK to reprint as is.

☐ Revision needed

   ☐ Rough layout attached
   ☐ Rough layout to follow
   ☐ _____

USAGE FOR NEXT 12 MONTHS

☐ Next 12 months same as last 12

☐ Increased to

☐ Decreased to

New monthly usage

☐ Form obsolete, replaced by:

_____

Explain below.

OTHER REMARKS

Approved By	Date

— No envelope needed for intraoffice mail —

**Fold over and
RETURN TO:**   **FORMS ADMINISTRATION**

Inactive Form Notice

Purpose

When a form has not been withdrawn from stock for a specified period of time, this form is used to find out from the requester whether the form is still active or is obsolete. If scrapping is requested, the inactive form notice serves as an order form to withdraw the material from stock, and as the accounting document to charge the cost of the forms to the user or some other charge code.

Construction

This is a four-part carbonless form, 8½″ × 11″. The copies are color-coded. One copy is sent to the office supply department, one serves as a packing list that accompanies the shipped material, one becomes a file copy for the forms group, and one is for the internal printshop's plate file, to be used for removing and destroying the plate, negatives, and so on.

Usage

The office supply department periodically reviews all forms inventories to find forms that have not been withdrawn from stock for a period of time (usually 18 months). Office supply enters the requester's name, department, and location in the appropriate place at the top of the form, along with information on the unused item. Inventory records are marked to indicate that an inactive notice has been prepared and sent to the forms group.

After receiving these notices from office supply, the forms group pulls the form's folder to see if it includes any illuminating information. If it is still necessary to check with the user, the first three parts of the form are sent to the requester through interoffice mail. The last part is kept in the form's folder as a record that the status is being questioned. When the form is returned by the requester with the reply section completed, the pink copy is removed and placed in the form's folder and the goldenrod copy, which had been in that folder as a control, is removed. If the form is obsolete, the goldenrod copy is sent to the printshop as a notification to remove the plate from their files. Regardless of the reply, the first two parts are returned to the office supply department. If some action is going to be taken with the material, these parts are used as the order and accounting document. If no action is to be taken, they are merely reviewed and destroyed.

INACTIVE FORM NOTICE
FORM

TO
Dept. - Bldg. - Floor

The Office Supply Department has informed us that the form listed has not been withdrawn from stock since the date shown.

To help us keep the inventory and our file current, please complete the following:

☐ Form is obsolete, replace by _____
　　　　　　　　　　　　　　　Form Number

　☐ Scrap balance on hand ⎫
　　　　　　　　　　　　　　⎬ _____
　☐ Send balance to: ⎭　　　Dept. Charge

☐ Form is still used. Average monthly usage _____

Form Title		
Form Number	Quantity in Stock	Unit
Stock Location	Unit Price $	Amount $
Last Withdrawal Date	Quantity Withdrawn	Dept. Number

Comments

Approved by ▶	Name - Dept. - Bldg.

If you are no longer responsible for this form, please return the notice immediately with the name and address of the responsible person below:

Notice should be sent to ▶	

Please think about this form, and all your forms.

Let's work together to find a better way.

We will be glad to discuss with you both forms control and paperwork simplification methods that you can use to improve your paperwork.

Thank you in advance for your cooperation in making sure that your function has all of the forms it needs, and none that it does not need.

If you have any questions please contact ▶		Phone

White — Office Supply　　　Canary — Packing List　　　Pink — F/A File　　　Goldenrod — Plate File
　　　　　　　　　　　　　　　　　Scrap Order

— No envelope needed for interoffice mail —

**Fold over and
RETURN TO:　FORMS ADMINISTRATION**

Print When Ordered (PWO) File Update

Purpose

This is, in a sense, an inactive notice on a form that is not stocked. Although there is no inventory to be destroyed, it still is necessary to update both the printshop files and the forms administration files.

Construction

This is a carbonless two-part unit set, 8½" × 8½". The original is sent to the requester, and the copy maintained as a reference in the form's file.

Usage

This form may originate in one of two ways. The printshop periodically reviews its plate files to find forms that have not been used for a two-year period. (The plate envelope is dated each time it is used.) It sends a list of the applicable form numbers to the forms group. This form is prepared from that list.

In addition, the forms group reviews its files periodically to find forms that have not been ordered for a two-year period, and this form is prepared as a result of that review. (A form's folder is marked with a "year" digit the first time it is used each calendar year.)

PRINT WHEN ORDERED (PWO)
FILE UPDATE

To
Dept. - Bldg. - Floor

Form

Form Title	Form No.	Date

Our records indicate that this form has not been printed within the last 2 years. To help us keep our files up to date, please complete

the following:

☐ Form is obsolete, replaced by _____

☐ Form is still used. Average monthly usage _____

Approved by ▶	Name - Dept. - Bldg.

If you are no longer responsible for this form, return the notice immediately,
with the name and address of the responsible person below:

Notice should be sent to ▶	

Please think about this form, and all your
forms.

Let's work together to find a better way.

We will be glad to discuss with you both
forms control and paperwork simplification
methods that you can use to improve your
paperwork.

Thank you in advance for your cooperation in making sure that your function has all
of the forms it needs, and none that it does not need.

If you have any questions, Please Contact ▶		Phone

— No envelope needed for interoffice mail —

Fold over and
RETURN TO   FORMS ADMINISTRATION

Outside Purchase Order Register

Purpose

This register is used to record all purchases of forms from outside suppliers. It provides a means of checking on the status of each order.

It is also used as the source document for preparation of a monthly activity report showing the number of new, revised, or reprint forms.

Construction

Like the form number register, this form should be printed on ledger stock, or a durable (70#) offset paper. It too should be hole-punched for maintenance in a three-ring binder. The form is a single sheet, 11″ × 8½″.

Usage

This form is completed in stages as the order flows through the purchasing and receiving functions.

At the time the requisition is sent to the purchasing agent, the forms analyst or order coordinator enters the current date; the form number; the analyst's initial in either the new, revised, or reprint column; an "X" in either the office supply (O/S), data processing (D/P), or direct (D) column; and the requested date for the order to be received in stock or delivered.

Later, when the purchase order copy or requisition is returned with the purchase order number shown, this number is recorded in the column labeled "P.O. No." This, of course, indicates that the purchasing function has been completed. If the purchase order number is missing, purchasing should be asked to check that the order is being processed properly.

When the forms group is notified of the receipt of the material, either by a packing list, form samples, or a receiving report, the date is entered in the date received column. A review of the two "date in stock" columns indicates how closely suppliers meet requested dates. If the receiving column is blank, then the material has not yet been received and some check should be made with the supplier.

At the end of the month, a tally of the check marks and initials in the new, revised, and reprint columns, and in the ship-to columns will provide the basic data needed for a monthly activity report of the forms group as it pertains to outside purchases. To simplify counting a large number of orders, note that there are 25 lines per column, a total of 50 lines per page.

OUTSIDE PURCHASE ORDER REGISTER

FORMS ADMINISTRATION

P.O. NO.	DATE	FORM NO.	NEW	REV	RPT	O/S	D/P	D	DATE IN STOCK	REQ.	REC.

OUTSIDE PURCHASE ORDER REGISTER

FORMS ADMINISTRATION

P.O. NO.	DATE	FORM NO.	NEW	REV	RPT	O/S	D/P	D	DATE IN STOCK	REQ.	REC.

Reproduction Job Number Register

Purpose

This form is the in-house equivalent of the outside purchase order register. All orders placed with the in-plant printshop are recorded here. The information is used to check on print orders and to develop monthly activity data.

Construction

This 11" × 8½" form should be printed on ledger paper or 70# offset paper (for durability) and should be maintained in a three-ring binder.

Usage

The analyst or coordinator enters the current date and form number and initials the new, revised, or reprint column. If the forms group assigns job numbers, this would be done when the order is entered. On this form, the last digit of the job number has been preprinted to save time and increase accuracy.

If the order is for a temporary form, which would not be numbered, the requester's department number is written in the right-hand column and no entry is made in the new, revised, or reprint column.

There is no special column on the form for the date that the form is received. A simple check mark can be placed to the left of the job number when an order is filled. Outstanding orders can be noted at a glance.

Activity information is tabulated monthly. There are 25 lines per column, representing 50 job orders per page.

REPRODUCTION JOB NUMBER REGISTER
FORMS ADMINISTRATION

JOB NO.	DATE	FORM NO.	NEW REV	REPT	TEMP. (DEPT. CODE)
1					
2					
3					
4					
5					
6					
7					
8					
9					
0					
1					
2					
3					
4					
5					
6					
7					
8					
9					
0					
1					
2					
3					
4					
5					

MONTH____

JOB NO.	DATE	FORM NO.	NEW REV	REPT	TEMP. (DEPT. CODE)
6					
7					
8					
9					
0					
1					
2					
3					
4					
5					
6					
7					
8					
9					
0					
1					
2					
3					
4					
5					
6					
7					
8					
9					
0					

Form Specifications

Purpose

The specification sheet provides the information needed by the manufacturer to properly construct and produce the form as ordered.

Construction

This 8½″ × 11″ form is a single sheet designed to be used as a master for photocopying. Suppliers are provided with a filled-in copy of the master for bidding or production.

Usage

Completing the specification sheet is an integral part of the design process. Most of the data elements on the spec sheet are self-explanatory, but some do need further elaboration:

• *Date Needed.* Always show an actual date. Don't say "Rush," "As soon as possible," or give any other vague time limit. "Rush" might mean 30 days to one supplier and 3 days to another.

• *For Copy, See.* When buying forms, the term copy refers to the layout of the form, not to a piece of paper. Depending on which box is checked, the copy should be attached to the specification sheet or would be available from the forms administration department.

• *Carbon Test Required.* This box is checked if the supplier is expected to provide a mock-up of the form, including the papers and carbons specified, for a test of the form's impression capability.

• *Form Size.* The width of a form is always specified first, followed by the length. Size indications should include all stubs and margins.

• *T L R B.* These are simply the abbreviations for top, left, right, and bottom. They are circled as appropriate to indicate areas for glue-ing, stapling, hole-punching, and so on. The area to the right of these indications is used to describe special construction characteristics of the continuous form.

• *Odd Size.* The form size indicated in the box below "Construction" should be the size of the largest part of the form. If any parts are smaller than that overall size, their sizes are entered in the odd-size column, and either W or L is circled. (As this odd size normally applies only to the dimension perpendicular to the stub of the form, it is rare to have odd sizes in both width and length of the same form.)

• *Copy Same As.* These two columns tell the forms manufacturer how many plates will be needed to produce this form. A check mark in the column indicates that a new plate is needed. It is preprinted for the first part because you would usually have a plate for the first part. If part two is the same as part one, the number "1" would be entered in the column for part two. If part three were different from parts one and two, a check mark would be entered in the column for part three. If part four were again the same as part one, "1" would be entered for part four. This is true for both the front and back of the form. If two colors of ink are used on one part, two check marks would be shown.

• *Ink.* If the ink is any color other than black, the number of the desired color is given in this column. There is such a great variety of colors available that it is unlikely you would get the one you wanted if you just specified red, green, blue, or yellow. Most printers use the Pantone matching system (PMS) to identify their ink colors.

• *Punch/Perf.* If special hole punches or perforations are necessary on a part, an "X" in either of these two columns refers the manufacturer to the "File Punch" or "Perforate" areas on spec sheet. If more space is needed for the explanations, use the "Special Instructions" area.

• *Carbon.* Indicate the carbon color and, if known, the carbon number for each piece of carbon paper to be included in the set. On this form, the carbon indication is written on the line for the part on which that carbon impression will appear.

• *File Punch.* If a normal three-ring punching is requested, simply circling the T, L, R, or B is sufficient. For other punch patterns, the number of holes, the diameter of those holes, and distance from the center of one hole to the center of the next must be indicated, as well as where holes should be placed (T, L, R, or B).

• *Perforate.* These instructions must indicate whether a vertical or horizontal perforation is needed, and the distance of the perforation from some point on the form, usually the left or top edge. Perforations are also shown on the layout.

• *Number.* If the form is to be serially numbered, a check in the "Yes" box and an indication of the starting number is all that is required. The layout should show where the number is to be applied.

• *"Crash" No.* A forms manufacturer can number the form either on the press or on the collator at the time the form is put together into a set. Forms numbered on the press have an individually printed number on each part. It is possible that these numbers would not be the same on every part of the set if there were any manufacturing problems. A "crash-numbered" form has the carbon or carbonless impression of the number on parts other than the first.

• *Preparation.* The manufacturer needs to know the method of preparation (that is, how the form will be filled out) so that the paper and carbon selected will produce the most legible form possible.

FORM SPECIFICATIONS

FORM

Form Title		Form Number — —
P.O. No.	Date Ordered	Date Needed	Quantity Ordered

This order is for:

- ☐ Exact Reprint - proof not required
- ☐ Revised Form - } Submit proof to
- ☐ New Form - } Forms Administration

For copy, see:

- ☐ Sample attached
- ☐ Forms Administration
- ☐ Carbon Test Required

Construction

Form Size W X L	
Sheets/Pd	Sets/Pd	Glue T L R B
Parts/Set	Stub "	Stub at: T L R B
Sets/Book		Staple at: T L R B
Cover		

- ☐ Pad
- ☐ Unit Set
- ☐ Book
- ☐ Other

☐ Continuous   Printer: _____   Other: _____

Marginal punches: ☐ Yes   ☐ No

Marginal perf. : ☐ No   ☐ Left _____"   ☐ Right _____"

Marginal fastening:

	L	R
Glue	L	R
Easy release glue	L	R
Crimp only	L	R
Crimp, with	L	R
Easy release glue		

Odd Size W or L	Paper Color	Paper Weight - Type	PART	Copy Same As or Chg (✔) Front	Back	Ink Color	Marginal Words	PUNCH	PERF	Carbon Color
			1	✔						
			2							
			3							
			4							
			5							
			6							
			7							
			8							
			9							
			10							
			11							
			12							

Special Instructions

FILE PUNCH	Std. 3 ring T L R B	No Holes Size	C to C	T L R B	PERFORATE
NUMBER	☐ Yes - start with ☐ No		☐ 'Crash' No.		Preparation ☐ Man. type. ☐ ☐ Handwritten ☐ Elec. type. ☐

Packing Instructions

Show on each label:

Form No., title, quantity, and Purchase Order or Release No.

Identify the carton that includes the packing list.

Use std. cartons & quantities (If continuous form, max. ctn. height of 12", unless exception approved)

Shipping Instructions

Send copy of packing list and 6 samples to:

Forms Administration

Ship to

Form Specifications—Reproduction

Purpose

This form is a specification sheet as well as a printshop job ticket. It is used for all forms ordered through the internal printshop.

Construction

This is an 11″ × 8½″ single-sheet form designed to be used as a master. Copies are produced each time an order is entered. The original is maintained in the form's folder.

Usage

If you have reviewed the other forms described in this section, then nearly all the information on this form will be self-explanatory. The additional items on this form provide space for information about composition and plates. These are necessary because the form will be used as a job ticket at the printshop.

In the area labeled "Paper," there are two sizes shown, run size and finish size. The latter is comparable to the overall size of the form, given with the width of the form first and the length last. Run size is the size of sheet to be used on the press. This size is determined and entered on the form by printshop personnel. After the first job is completed, the form's order coordinator records the indicated run size on the master and it is then reproduced on copies from that point on, for use by the printshop.

If the forms are to be numbered, forms administration enters the beginning number in the "Serial Numbers" section. Because exact quantities are not always known, after the job is completed the printshop records the last number assigned. In most cases, the number that would follow that one becomes the beginning serial number on the next job.

FORM SPECIFICATION — REPRODUCTION

FORM

Form Title

Form No.

Serial Number

Job Number	Charge Code			Quantity	Date Ordered	Compl. Date	New	Rev	Rpt	By	Comments	From (F/A)	To (Repro.)
	Cont	Main	Sub	Proj. - Class									

Requester

Proof to (NEW or REV. only)
FORMS ADMINISTRATION

Samples to:
FORMS ADMINISTRATION
AND:

Ship to:
☐ Stock
☐ Other →

COMPOSITION

- Photo Composer Text
- Photo Composer Headliner
- IBM Composer
- Paste-up Proof
- Color-Key Proof

PLATES

- Photo plate
- Camera plate
- Paper plate
- Snap plate
- Typeset

No. Plates | Print Up

PAPER

	Run Size	Wgt.	Color	Description	Finish Size
IBM Composer	X				X
Paste-up Proof	X				X
Photo plate	X				X
Camera plate	X				X
Paper plate	X				X
Typeset	X				X

Press Operator | Repro. Supv.

Special Instructions

INK

Black ↑

PRINT

- Front Only
- Front and Back
  - ☐ Same
  - ☐ Diff.
  - ☐ Tumblehead
  - ☐ Head-to-Head
  - ☐ Side-to-Head

BINDERY

		Shts./Set	No. Sets	Shts./Set	Chip	Binding at				Pad at
Sets						T	L	R	B	
Pads	No. Sheets					T	L	R	B	
Books	Cover							Staples at		
Punch	3-ring	Holes	Diam.			T	L	R	B	C to C
Perf.						T	L	R	B	From
Score						T	L	R	B	From
Fold						T	L	R	B	From
Number	—See Above—									
Wrap	per pkg.									

Repro. Dept. Material Charge

Monthly Activity Report

Purpose
This report indicates the workload and output of the forms group. Although activity figures can be misleading and are sometimes misused, they are necessary to help determine proper staff levels.

Construction
This is an 11″ × 8½″ form, printed on 70# offset paper.

Usage
At the end of the month, the two order registers discussed earlier in this chapter are reviewed and tallied. Comparative figures for the same month last year and for the year to date are entered. The lower right-hand corner can be used for comments about the month's activity.

Copies are made for the forms analysts and for the middle manager to whom the forms manager reports.

If the forms group is broken down into several smaller units, a report can be prepared for each unit and then combined for the overall department.

MONTHLY ACTIVITY REPORT
FORMS ADMINISTRATION

FORM _____

Month _____

FORMS ORDERS

Type of Order	Reproduction		Outside Purchases			Total Month	This Year-To-Date				Last Year-To-Date			
	Stock	Direct	Stock	Direct	DP		Stock	Direct	DP	Total	Stock	Direct	DP	Total
New														
Revisions														
Reprints														
Temporarys	—		—		—		—		—			—		—	
Total														
Same Month Last Year														
Percent change from Last Year							%	%	%	%				

NUMBER OF FORMS IN USE

	This Month	Year-To-Date	Last Year-To-Date
Beginning Count			
Additions			
Obsoletions			
Ending Count			

Layout Sheets

Purpose

Layout sheets are designed to help the analyst or designer produce a good layout of a form.

Construction

These should be printed on 70# offset paper. One is an 11″ × 8½″ sheet, the other is 8½″ × 11″. The vertical space between lines is ¹/₆″, the horizontal space is ¹/₅″. The forms should be printed with about a 5- or 10-percent screen using blue ink.

Usage

Larger, specialized layout pads are usually available at no charge from forms suppliers, but most of the forms you design will fit on the conveniently sized sheets shown here. After the design work is finished, it is easy to make copies of the layout for review by the requester and any other interested parties. The light blue lines will not show up on the copies, so it will be easier for them to imagine what the finished form will look like.

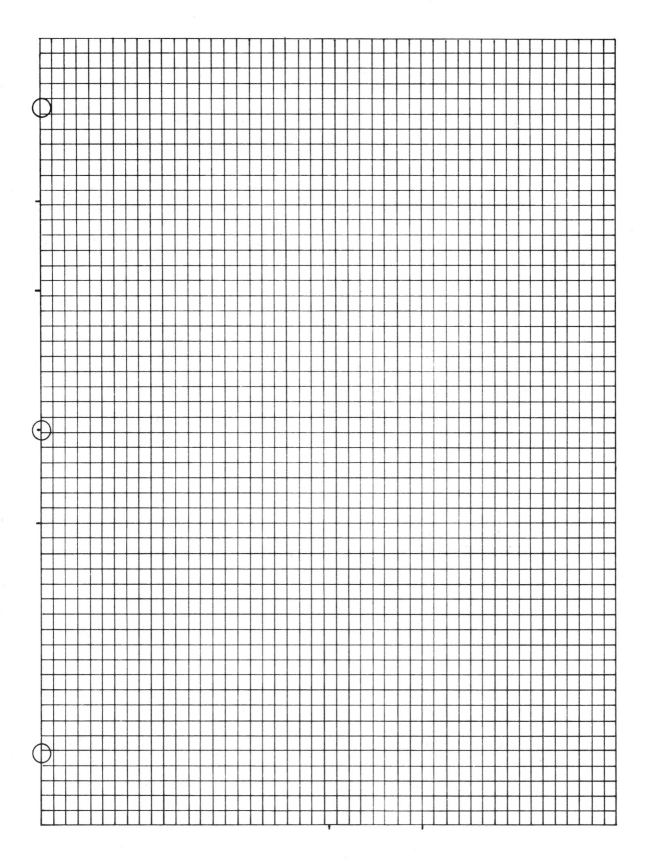

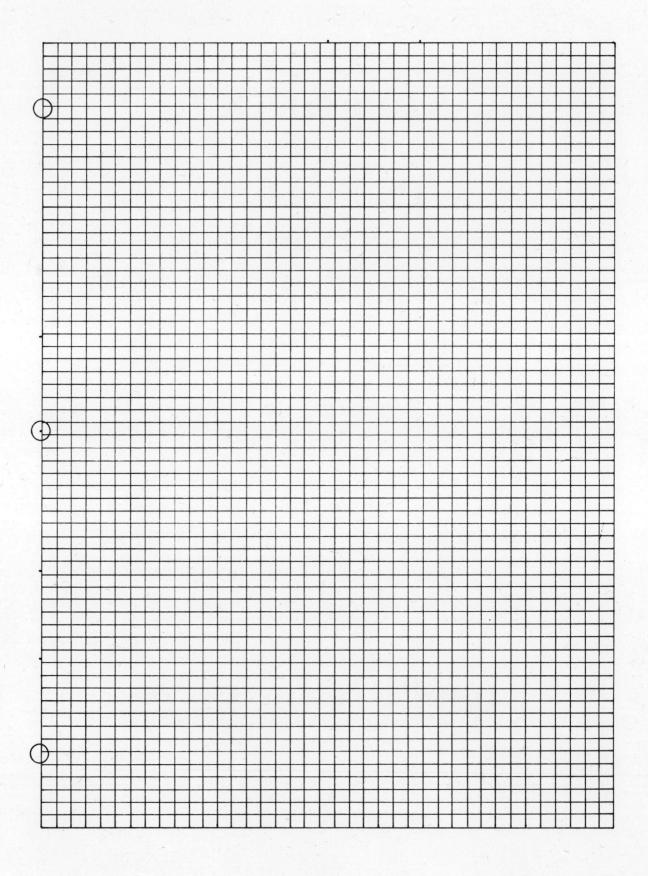

APPENDIX I

Personnel Requirements of Forms Administration

SOME departments in an organization are ideal for breaking in new employees and preparing them for promotion to other areas—but not forms administration. People working in the management, analysis, and design of forms must have the background, experience, and ability to earn the respect of those they are dealing with. Experienced employees who are familiar with the organization are more likely to fill these requirements.

The activities of forms administration personnel are described here as if each were a full-time job for one or more people. This is true of such jobs in a large organization. In smaller companies, some duties will be combined. Perhaps one person will handle all of them, maybe even on a part-time basis. But, regardless of the number of people, the number of forms, the size of the organization, or the kind of organization, the requirements and activities remain the same.

The three basic categories of positions in forms administration are clerical, analytical, and management. Sample position descriptions of each follow. They are intended to be general; each will have to be carefully reviewed and revised to fit circumstances of specific organizations.

Education requirements are not shown in the descriptions. They often result in the unwarranted exclusion of some candidates, and no positive, direct connection can be shown between educational level and job performance. However, a person qualified as a forms manager usually has an undergraduate degree and some experience in the organization; a qualified analyst usually has some college background and experience within the organization, and an order coordinator usually has a high school education and experience within the organization.

Selecting the right people and determining the appropriate salary range is critical to the continuing success of *any* department—forms administration is no exception. The appropriate salary range for an analyst performing the job described would be comparable to a data processing systems analyst. Order coordinators would be properly classified about one step higher than a secretary. Forms managers would be classified and paid the same as any other department heads.

Forms Administration Manager
Position Description

A. *Purpose*

To formulate and direct the organization's forms administration program, which services all line and staff departments, including subsidiaries

B. *Objectives*

1. To manage the forms administration department and coordinate its operations with related departments to analyze, properly design, and arrange for production or procurement of all forms used by the organization. Must consider the following:
   (a) Need for the form and information
   (b) Clerical efficiency in the total use of the form
   (c) Consistency of information
   (d) Proper retention or destruction capabilities and procedures
   (e) Inventory levels, distribution, and form obsolescence
   (f) Reproduction capability
   (g) Economy in production and use
2. Improve the effectiveness and efficiency of paperwork methods and systems related to forms and other records by considering the latest techniques, office mechanization, and integrated operation

154

C. *Duties*
  1. General management of the department
      (a) Establish short- and long-range objectives, secure management approval, and follow up to meet goals
      (b) Prepare short- and long-range forecasts of department expenditures and organization-wide expenses in related areas
      (c) Establish policies and procedures for effective operation of department
      (d) Develop activity and progress reports for control of department and follow-up of programs
      (e) Select and train necessary personnel to carry out the departmental responsibilities
      (f) Develop personnel and job structures to provide opportunities for promotion
      (g) Be informed on related operations in other organizations, for applications to own department
  2. Management of the forms function
      (a) Familiarize management and department heads with the purpose and services of forms administration
      (b) Develop and update forms administration information, including policy, procedures, and standards, for organization-wide use
      (c) Educate personnel on the services and techniques available for development of productive and effective paperwork
      (d) Maintain a cooperative working relationship with all groups involved in paperwork processing, systems development, and forms procurement or production
      (e) Establish analysis techniques to:
          • Strive for integrated use of recorded data by consolidating forms
          • Clarify and standardize forms to provide consistent information for accounting and other company records
          • Obtain clearance when necessary from legal, advertising, personnel, and other staff groups on matters affecting organizational policy, use of logos, disclaimer clauses, and employee relations
      (f) Establish design and specification standards
      (g) Implement a system to determine reorder points and quantities
      (h) Determine and update criteria for deciding on internal reproduction vs. outside procurement
      (i) Provide for periodic analysis of usage, costs, types, constructions, and so on for combining orders or for contract buying
      (j) Arrange for periodic analysis of each form to determine its current status concerning usage, design, and so on

155

(k) Update self, department personnel, and others concerned with new techniques, concepts, and developments in forms analysis and design, records management, reproduction, printing, duplicating, copying, and business equipment

D. *Knowledge, Abilities, and Skills Required*

1. Management/supervisory capability
2. Familiarity with company organization, policies, and products
3. Accounting knowledge and application
4. Office and factory clerical systems and procedures
5. Methods analysis techniques
6. Understand cost factors relating to forms usage and retention
7. Printing, reproduction, and duplicating processes, and machines used to produce and copy forms
8. Paper, carbon paper, and ink standards
9. Filing equipment, systems, and techniques
10. Microfilm equipment, systems, and techniques
11. Business machines and other mechanical systems
12. Operation and needs of a data processing center
13. Sense of design and layout
14. Printing trade procurement customs
15. Typography, composition, and platemaking processes
16. Forms construction possibilities
17. Internal reproduction operations
18. Procurement practices, techniques, and procedures

E. *Personal Qualities*

1. Neat and orderly
2. Intelligent, tactful, with common sense
3. Perseverant
4. Persuasive
5. Perceptive
6. Attentive to detail, accurate, and precise
7. Resourceful, imaginative, creative
8. Good communicator
9. Potential to absorb additional responsibilities coincident with growth of the organization

F. *Contacts*

1. Printing company representatives
2. Purchasing agent
3. Reproduction and office supply departments
4. Corporate and division systems personnel
5. Data processing personnel
6. Department managers
7. Associates in other organizations in surrounding area and nationwide

G. *Effect on Expenditures and Savings*
1. About 30 percent of the average working hour is spent processing forms. Properly analyzed and designed forms will reduce the related clerical processing costs by:
   (a) being easier to fill in and use
   (b) reducing the chance of error
   (c) providing consistent information
   (d) creating a better mental attitude
2. Properly designed and analyzed forms will minimize printing costs by using:
   (a) the right paper
   (b) the right standard size
   (c) the right number of parts
   (d) the right ink, and so forth
3. Properly controlled forms will minimize printing, procurement, and inventory costs by ordering correct quantities at the right time, and by considering usage, quantity discounts, revision probability, and current inventory

H. *Supervision*
1. Direct supervision of analytical and clerical staff
2. Functional relationship with personnel serving in part-time forms coordinating positions in other departments or locations.

Forms Analyst
Position Description

A. *Purpose*
To help all parts of the organization develop and improve their forms and related paperwork systems in order to reduce administrative costs by minimizing the clerical effort needed, maximizing the informational benefits received, and minimizing the cost of the forms

B. *Duties*
1. Work with forms users to develop the best paperwork system to fill their requirements; analyze the need for the information, determine the best method of preparation, distribution, filing, and so on, and propose changes to new or existing systems
2. Design the forms needed to allow the system to function efficiently, accurately, and in a timely manner
3. Obtain and maintain the supply of printed forms; determine the source (in-house or outside), quantity, inventory location, reorder point, construction specifications (based on usage amount, inventory

on hand, quantity discounts, obsolescence probability, and printers' capabilities)

C. *Knowledge, Abilities, and Skills Required*
1. Organization policies
2. Systems analysis techniques
3. Printing methods, techniques, and practices
4. Understand manual and computer systems including applicable machines
5. Communications skills: presenting, listening, and understanding
6. Salesmanship (to sell ideas)
7. Forms design ability
    (a) Sense of design and layout
    (b) Paper and ink standards
    (c) Forms construction
    (d) Precise, neat, legible layout preparation

D. *Personal Qualities*
1. Neat and orderly
2. Intelligent, tactful, with common sense
3. Perseverant
4. Persuasive
5. Perceptive
6. Attentive to detail, accurate, precise
7. Resourceful, imaginative, creative
8. Good communicator: speaking, writing, listening, and understanding

E. *Contacts*
Problem-solving interactions with personnel from all parts of the organization, all job levels, and all educational backgrounds, and with forms suppliers

F. *Effect on Expenditures and Savings*
Efficiency, accuracy, and availability of forms and related clerical processing have a substantial effect on operating expenses and on the ability to assemble proper management information for action or decision

Forms Order Coordinator
Position Description

A. *Purpose*
To assist the forms analyst(s) in satisfying the complete forms requirements of the organization by initiating, controlling, and following up on all orders for forms, from any supplier (in-house or outside), and by helping in other ways as needed

B. *Duties*
1. Calculate reorder points and reorder quantities on all forms up for reorder
2. Contact users for approval to reprint or revise forms at the reorder point
3. Prepare and assemble the paperwork needed for each order (inside job ticket or purchase requisition, specifications, sample or layout) and enter the order
4. Record and update order registers, follow up on exceptions
5. Review and discuss specifications with suppliers
6. Expedite orders as needed
7. Maintain forms files
8. Handle inquiries, complaints, and so on by phone, mail, wire, or visit
9. Type reports or correspondence as needed
10. Assist analyst in other areas as needed.

C. *Knowledge, Abilities, and Skills Required*
1. Tact and diplomacy
2. Communications skills
3. Ability to make routine decisions in both normal and exceptional situations
4. Printing methods, techniques, and practices
5. Normal office skills (typing, filing, copying, and so on)
6. Attention to detail, accurate, precise

D. *Contacts*
Most contacts are problem-solving, non-routine interactions with people from other departments or with suppliers

E. *Effect on Expenditures and Savings*
Accuracy and timeliness of ordering/reordering affects the cost of forms and the efficiency of clerical operations throughout the organization

APPENDIX II

Glossary of Terms

IN every line of work, some unique words or phrases are used to describe various things or actions peculiar to that field. This jargon is familiar to experienced workers in the field, but can be very confusing to newcomers or lay people. The following list covers many of the terms used every day by analysts, designers, buyers, and printers. It is intended to help clarify communication among us as we go about our duties of helping others improve their information flow.

This glossary is not complete, and the definitions are not always technical in nature. These are the terms I am familiar with, and the meanings that I have come to associate with those terms over a period of years.

alignment mark   a mark preprinted on a form to assist the user (usually a computer operator) to position the form correctly for the first entry.

AMS   Administrative Management Society

area carbon   *see* patterned carbon

ARMA   Association of Records Managers and Administrators

ASM   Association for Systems Management

backer   *see* back printing

back printing   printing that appears on the reverse side of a sheet, usually information less important to the reader

ballot box   a small box located next to each answer for the user to indicate the selected answer out of a series

bar code   a coding system using vertical bars printed or stamped on a sheet to be read by a bar code reader

basic sheet size   the size of paper used to determine the substance weight; 17″ × 22″ for bond paper

basis weight or basic weight   the weight, in pounds, of a ream of paper cut to a standard sheet size

between-set perforations   perforations on continuous forms that separate the bottom of one form from the top of the next

BFMA   Business Forms Management Association

binder   for our purposes, any device for holding forms or other records together after they have been used, such as a three-ring binder

bindery operations   in forms manufacturing, operations taking place after printing, including punching, perforating, folding, slitting, cutting, trimming, and numbering

binding   on forms, the portion or edge of a group of forms that is bound with padding, staples, etc.

blanket   a rubber-coated sheet wrapped around a cylinder that transfers the image from the plate to the paper

bleed   to extend the printed image to the edge of the paper; also, the unwanted transfer of carbon chemicals to the regular paper in the form

blockout   a printed pattern used to hide a carbon impression in selected areas of specific copies of a form

body   the main portion of a printed form, as compared with the title or instructions

boldface   a style of type (available as a version of all common typefaces) that is heavier and darker than regular type

bond paper   writing paper used where strength and durability are important, such as in forms

book   a group of forms bound at one edge, usually stapled

bootleg   a form not properly ordered through a forms group

bottom stub   a glued stub at the bottom, or foot, of a form with unit-set construction; sometimes specified on typed forms for easy erasing, even though it does not feed well around the platen of the typewriter

box design   *see* ULC design

brightness   a paper characteristic, measured in terms of reflectance; important for OCR forms

bug   a manufacturer's identification mark, a union mark, or an organization's logo

burn   to expose a photo-offset plate to the negative

burster   a device for separating continuous forms between sets

butt roll   a roll of paper that has been almost all used

calender   a series of horizontal cast-iron rollers at the end of the paper machine through which the paper is passed to increase the smoothness of the surface

caliper the thickness of a sheet of paper, expressed in mils

camera-ready copy artwork or layout ready to be photographed for photo-offset reproduction without further alteration

caps capital letters

caption word or phrase associated with a single field on a form

carbon paper with a pigmented coating that is used to transfer an image through pressure or impact

carbon-interleaved continuous or unit-set forms with one-time carbon paper included between the plies

carbonize to coat the back of regular forms paper with a carbon coating, usually with a spot or pattern for selective imaging

carbonless paper paper that is specially manufactured or coated to provide transfer of impression to multiple parts without the use of carbon paper; often incorrectly called NCR paper

card *see* tab card

cathode ray tube (CRT) a TV-type tube and screen, usually with a typewriter-style keyboard, for computer input and output

CB carbonless paper with a coating on the back; used as the top sheet in a set

CF carbonless paper with a coating on the front; used as the last sheet in a set

CFB carbonless paper with a coating on both the front and back; used for all interior parts

character printer a machine that prints one character at a time, such as a typewriter

check digit a suffix digit added to a number to create a certain total when the digits are manipulated according to a specified formula, to reduce transposition errors, and so on

chemical carbonless carbonless paper that transfers an image when two chemicals are mated; usually prepared with a chemical on the back of one sheet and another chemical on the front of the next (*see also* CB, CF, and CFB)

Chinese blockout *see* blockout

chip strip a ¼″ strip between some continuous tab cards that is a result of the manufacturing method that produces long grain cards

clay coating a surface coating on bond paper that increases opacity and smoothness; often used in magazines

clear area the uncoated portion of a patterned carbon

clear-edge carbon carbon with a narrow strip of clear tissue along an edge, which gives a clean edge for removal (*also called* feather-edge carbon)

cold type type other than hot lead or raised image type; set by a machine,

163

such as a Varityper or Selectric composer, that produces a photographic image of the material for offset printing (*see also* photocomposition)

collate   to assemble and arrange in proper order the various parts of a set

collator   machine that collates parts of a form, either in sheets or rolls, and sometimes numbers, punches, perforates, or folds the completed set

colors: standard sequence   unit sets of up to four parts are usually arranged: white, canary, pink, goldenrod

column   a vertical strip on a form for entry of a series of similar items

column heading   the title of a column; similar to a caption except that it applies to more than one entry

COM   computer output microfilm

combination run   two or more print jobs run together to save money

combined order   forms ordered together to take advantage of lower prices for a combination run

composer   machine similar to a typewriter, used to prepare camera-ready copy for forms

composition   the process of setting copy in type

continuous form   form manufactured from a continuous web (roll) and not cut apart before use; usually perforated between sets; most often folded by a forms suppliers, but may be rolled for use on some equipment

continuous unit set   a continuous form with one margin area glued to provide a unit set after bursting

control numbering   number usually put in the margin or stub area by the supplier to monitor the quantity produced

copy   material furnished to be used in production of printed material, such as a form layout; also, sometimes used as a synonym for a part or ply

copy change   a difference in material to be printed on different parts of a set; also, change in the copy after proofs have been prepared

corner cut   an angled cut on one corner of a tab card used to help maintain cards correctly in the deck

crash numbering   consecutive numbering using either a carbon or a carbonless impression for images on all parts other than the original

crash perforation   perforation done by a collator that cuts through all parts of a set at one time

crash printing   printing done with a raised-image plate that produces a carbon or carbonless image of the format on parts other than the first

crimp   a temporary and flexible fastening in which fingers of paper are pushed through the parts being fastened together (*see also* firm fastening, flexible fastening)

cross-perforations   *see* between-set perforations

custom form   a form manufactured to a customer's specifications, as compared with a stock form taken out of inventory

cut an element of the form, such as a picture or logo, that has been prepared for plate-making by some special process, such as etching or engraving

cut forms single-sheet forms

cutoff the circumference of the cylinder on a rotary press or collator

cylinder gap *see* lockup space

dealer a firm selling business forms that does not print those forms

decollator equipment that separates the parts, including carbon paper, of a continuous form

deleaver equipment that removes the carbon paper from a continuous form

delete to remove copy, type, or parts of a layout, or to direct the compositor to do so

density the blackness or darkness of an image

depth dimension parallel with the marginal punching on a continuous form

desensitize to coat the surface of carbonless paper to eliminate the imaging from an area, as with a patterned carbon; done on the press by the forms manufacturer

die-cut to remove a section of paper with a two-piece die set; used to prepare windows, special non-round holes, and so on

dimensional stability the ability of paper to maintain its size during manufacturing and through changes in temperature or humidity

dingbat a typographical ornament, such as a star, arrow, or circle, used to attract attention to certain lines, words, or portions of a form

direct-image master a duplicating master that can be typed or drawn on directly, rather than produced photographically

distribution the routing of parts of a form after it has been prepared

Ditto a trade name, often used incorrectly as a general term for spirit duplicating

double-faced carbon carbon paper coated on both sides, often patterned, for forms requiring two-sided entries

double hairline a pair composed of two narrow lines set very close together

double stub a unit set containing two stubs; for use as two sets after initial preparation

drilling punching holes through a stack of forms off the press, rather than punching holes through individual forms on the press

dropout a color that does not reproduce photographically

dropped stub a perforation at the glued stub of a unit set that is lower than the other perforations, so that a portion of that part stays with the stub; used to withhold information or to adjust the part size

dummy a sample mock-up set of papers and carbons, often used to test their imaging capability on a specific machine

Dycril a trade name (Du Pont) for a plate that develops a raised image for printing

edge padding a padding compound (glue) brushed on one edge of a group of sets or sheets to make pads or unit sets

edge-punched card a card with holes punched along all four sides that is sorted with a long needle

elite 12-character-per-inch typewriter spacing

entry a unit of data or information written on a form as it is used

EOQ economic order quantity; used in inventory calculations

face the front side of a form

facsimile the exact reproduction of something, such as a signature

facsimile transmission the sending of a facsimile by wire or radio

fanapart glue padding compound used to make carbonless unit sets; designed to not adhere to uncoated surfaces of carbonless paper (the top of the first sheet and bottom of the last sheet)

fan set a carbonless unit set with edge padding rather than a glued stub

fastening the method of holding continuous forms together

feather edge the clear uncoated edge of carbon paper, usually used to give a clean pulling surface for carbon removal (*also called* clear edge)

felt side the top side of a sheet of paper; the best side for printing (*see also* wire side)

field an area of a form allocated to a specific item; usually refers to the horizontal space requirement

file holes holes for binding a form in a filing device, such as a three-ring binder

filling-up a condition in which spaces between the dots of a screen fill up with ink

fill-in space a blank area of a form for user entry of requested information

film positive a normal-appearing positive image on film (rather than a negative) used for proofing and for projection transparencies

firm fastening fastening of continuous forms that does not allow the plies to shift, as they do with a crimp (*see also* crimp, flexible fastening)

flat a large sheet with negatives assembled on it preparatory to plate-making

flat charge a one-time charge for preparatory work, negatives, plates, press makeready, and so on

flat forms same as single-sheet forms or cut forms

flexible fastening fastening of continuous forms that allows plies to shift (*see also* crimp, firm fastening)

flowchart a representation of a procedure that usually uses symbols, lines, and arrows to follow the movement of people, paperwork, and so on

flush *see* justify

FOB freight on board; refers to point at which ownership changes and (usually) freight is paid for by the shipper

fold mark a line or symbol printed on a form as a guide to the user, especially for window envelope insertion or self-mailers

font a complete assortment of a given size and style of type

foot the bottom edge of a form

form any sheet designed for recording specific data, usually with preprinted headings, captions, lines, boxes, or other devices to guide the entry, subsequent interpretation, and use of that information

fourdrinier name of a papermaking machine, after the Fourdriniers who financed the first such machine in 1803

fugitive glue similar to rubber cement, used to temporarily fasten forms

full-coated carbon carbon paper coated completely, as compared to patterned or strip carbon

gap space *see* lockup space

generation a transfer of an image from one sheet to another, with each successive transfer being referred to as the next generation

grain direction the primary direction of the fibers in paper: fibers are parallel to the length of the roll as it is produced; therefore, they are parallel to the marginal punches on a continuous form and to the stub on a "web-press produced" unit set

grain, long the grain running parallel with the longest dimension of the sheet

grain, short the grain running parallel with the shortest dimension of the sheet

gripper margin the leading edge of a sheet on a sheet-fed press; cannot be printed upon; usually measures ⅜″ to ½″

guaranteed numbering a user requirement that consecutively numbered forms be supplied without any missing numbers

guillotine a paper cutter used in bindery operations

gum sometimes refers to edge padding compound or adhesive on labels

hairline a very thin rule, the type of line used most often on forms

halftone a reproduction of a photograph in which the image is formed by dots of various sizes

head the top of a form as it is normally read or used

head-to-foot relationship between front and back printing in which the top of the back printing is opposite the bottom of the front

head-to-head the relationship between front and back printing on a form in which a normal book-type arrangement is used

head-to-side relationship between front and back printing in which printing on the two sides is at right angles to each other

hot-melt glue glue used for fastening continuous or unit-set forms; it sets very fast, allowing high-speed fastening

hot-spot carbonizing applying carbon to parts of the back of a form for selective imaging without carbon paper; done on the press by the forms manufacturer

IBFI International Business Forms Industries

impression one revolution of a forms press; or, the printing of one sheet; or, the image of entries on multiple parts of a form

imprint a second printing in an area, normally used for names and addresses; can be done on a press or with an imprinter of some sort

imprinter a device for imprinting, such as for credit card charge slips

index a card-weight sheet, used for index cards, postcards, and so on

in-plant shop normally refers to a "captive" printshop, one that prints material only for a single organization (*also called* in-house shop)

IPMA In-Plant Printing Management Association

italic a slanted version of a typeface, often used for emphasis

item a unit of data to be entered on a form

jog to align sheets of paper in a stack, especially before cutting or padding

justify to space out lines evenly to a specified measure to produce an even margin on the left or right

Kardex a trademark for one version of a visible card file, often used for inventory control

Keysort card a McBee trademark for a card system with punched holes around the edges for sorting with a pin or needle

kraft paper or board made from unbleached wood pulp, brown in color

layout a drawing of a form

layout sheet a sheet with preprinted grid lines to help the designer prepare a layout

leader a type of line, usually dotted or dashed, used to guide one's eyes across the page

leading zeros zeros preceding the first significant digit of a number

lead time the time required to produce a form before it will be available for use

ledger stock a grade of paper generally used for records that are relatively permanent and subject to repeated handling

length on continuous forms, the distance between the cross-perforations, or, from top to bottom on the form

letterpress a printing process that uses a raised image that is inked and then comes into direct contact with the paper

line copy copy consisting of only solid blacks and whites, as compared to screened or halftone areas

line holes the punched holes along the margins of a continuous form (*see also* marginal punches)

line printer a printer that prints an entire line at one time; includes most computer printers

lithography an offset printing process that uses a flat surfaced plate

lockup space an image-free area on a form ⅜″ to ½″ wide, running at right angles to the marginal punches or stub; required by the mechanism that holds the plate on the cylinder

logotype the name of an organization or product in a special characteristic design, also referred to as simply "logo"

loose perforation a perforation that is easy to tear along

lowercase letters the small letters of the alphabet, as compared to the capital, or uppercase, letters

M abbreviation for 1,000

makeready tasks that must be done preparatory to beginning a print job

marginal perforation vertical perforations along the margins of a continuous form that allow easy removal of the marginal punches

marginal punches a series of holes along the vertical edges of a continuous form that are used to control the form as it is moved through a computer printer or similar equipment

marginal words words or phrases printed on multiple-part sets that give instructions about distribution to the users; can be changed from part to part, usually at no cost to the buyer

mark reading, mark sensing the mechanical recognition of bars or other marks on a form using the magnetic or conductive properties of the mark

matrix printer a printing unit that forms each character from a series or pattern of dots, much like an electric scoreboard does

maximum line length the longest line that can be written by the printing device; on a typewriter, determined by the width of the carriage, on a computer printer, by the number of type positions built into the machine for each line

mechanical camera-ready copy that has been pasted up into final format, ready to be shot

mechanical transfer carbonless paper with a grayish coating on the back that transfers to the next sheet in much the same way carbon paper transfers an impression

MICR magnetic ink character recognition; the system widely used by banks for automatically processing checks and other related paperwork

microfilm film used for storage of records; usually comes as 16mm rolls or cartridges, or as microfiche (many images on the same film)

mil a measurement used for thickness, $\frac{1}{1,000}$″

Mimeograph a trademark of the A.B. Dick Company for its stencil duplicating process

multi-web press a press capable of printing several rolls of paper at the same time, usually collating them in the same operation

narrow carbon any carbon narrower than the form it is used on; usually found in continuous sets

NBFA National Business Forms Association

NCR often used to mean carbonless paper, but is the trademark of Appleton Papers for its brand of carbonless paper

negative a photographic image on film in which black images are transparent and white areas are opaque; used in preparing an offset plate

non-freeze carbon specially formulated carbon paper for forms used in conditions of freezing temperatures such as at service stations or fuel delivery trucks

non-impact printer a computer printout unit that forms images and prints them on paper without type bars or other impact devices (described further in Chapter 6, "Designing Forms for Automation")

non-processed carbon carbon paper (used in continuous forms) that has not undergone any processing, other than slitting after its manufacture; normally about ¾″ narrower than the form because it does not have marginal punches; usually requires glueing to hold it in place

non-reflective ink ink that is read by an optical scanner

non-reproducing colors inks, such as light blue, that will not reproduce photographically

numbering machine a device mounted on the press or collator to serially number the forms; available in various heights and for varying number of digits

OCR optical character recognition; the machine reading of characters by their shapes

offset printing a printing system using a flat plate, usually with a photographically produced image, that transfers the inked image to an intermediate roll (blanket) and then to the material being printed on

one-time carbon carbon designed to be used once and thrown away, which is the type of carbon typically used in forms today

onionskin a very lightweight bond paper often used where many copies are needed

on-line a computer system in which the user's terminal is hooked up directly with the computer, giving immediate update and inquiry capabilities

opacity the property of paper that minimizes the amount of show-through from one side to the other

opaque the process of covering up areas on a negative not wanted on a plate

opposite direction sometimes used to define the dimension that runs at right angles to the stub of a unit set

170

optical scanner   the computer input device that reads numbers or letters on a sheet and converts them to machine-usable codes

outlook envelope   a window envelope

overlay   a transparent or translucent flap placed over the copy or mechanical showing colors, breaks, instructions, or corrections

overrun   the quantity over the amount specified on a forms order that is produced; trade practices allow a 10 percent over- or under-factor to allow for production variables (*see also* underrun)

Ozalid   a trademark of GAF often improperly used as a generic name for the diazo copying process

padded forms   single sheets held together at one edge with a padding compound or glue

pantograph   a background pattern, usually of screens, symbols, or logos, on documents such as checks and certificates

paper master   a paper printing plate used on an offset duplicator in which the image was made by typing or hand lettering

parallel perforation   a perforation running parallel with the stub of a unit set

part   one ply or sheet of a multiple-part form

pasteup   the assembly of copy for photographic reproduction as needed for the printing process (*see also* camera-ready copy)

patterned carbon   carbon coated with a pattern other than a strip running parallel with the roll, produced with a process more like printing than coating

pegboard form   a form designed for simple accounting systems, using a board with a series of pins along the edge to control single sheets of related forms, used in a shingled arrangement

pencil carbon   carbon made to transfer the image best when the pressure is applied with a gliding motion, as compared with the impact of a typewriter; usually produced in a blue color

perforating blade   a notched cutting blade mounted on the press or collator for cutting perforations at right angles to the movement of paper

perforating wheel   a slotted, notched blade used to cut perforations parallel with the movement of paper

perforation   a series of cuts or holes in a form to weaken it for separation or tearing

perforation tear strength   for the user, best described as easy or hard to tear; for the manufacturer, described in terms of the number of ties per inch, or the number of cuts per inch

per M   (per thousand) the units used to express the price of forms

permanent fastening   fastening continuous forms so that they will not come apart without tearing the paper; usually used to produce unit sets after the continuous form is burst

phantom   a light image, usually screened; often used for decorative purposes

photocomposition   the creation of an image by exposure of characters onto a light-sensitive material, for use in offset printing (*see also* cold type)

Photostat   name of a firm that manufactures copying and printing equipment; improperly used as a generic term for a photocopy

pica   a printer's measure, equivalent to 12 points; also used to indicate a typewriter spacing of ten characters per inch

pinfeed platen   a platen with sprocket-type mechanisms at each end to control the movement of the forms

pitch   term for the horizontal spacing of a typewriter or printer; a pica typewriter would be 10 pitch

plate   the surface from which printing is done in a press or duplicator; can be plastic, paper, metal, or rubber

platen   the rubber-covered cylinder around which a form is passed for writing, such as on a typewriter

point   the printer's basic unit of measure, equal to .013837″ (approximately $1/72''$); also, a measure of thickness for certain paper stocks, where it equals .001″

position   a horizontal space for a character on a form

precollated paper   sheet stock that has been collated at the mill in certain color sequences, used primarily for production of carbonless unit sets in in-plant printshops

press   a device used to perform printing

press depth   an even division of the circumference of a printing cylinder, which determines the form sizes possible for a given press

press perforation   perforation cut by a blade or wheel on the press

press proof   a sheet taken from the actual press run for a final proofing of the copy; not a usual practice with forms

pressure sensitive   material with an adhesive coating protected by a peel-off liner; usually used for labels

printer   a writing machine that operates under machine control, as a computer printer

printout   information which has been printed by a printer, such as a computer printout on a continuous form

processed carbon   carbon paper that has been punched or perforated before being collated with a continuous form

proof   a copy of typeset material provided so that the layout can be checked for accuracy

pull-out margin   the area, provided by using short carbons, that the user grasps to separate the unit-set plies from the stub and carbon paper

punch, punching   a hole, or series of holes, put in a form

punched card   *see* tab card

ream 500 sheets of paper

recurring data information written on two or more forms in the same processing sequence

reflectance the paper characteristic indicating the amount of light reflected from different angles, which is especially important for optical scanning

reflective ink ink that has the same reflective qualities as paper, so that it will not be read by a scanner

register a type of lightweight bond paper designed for computer output forms

registration the alignment of one part of a form with another

reverse print printing done so that the background is printed and the copy is left blank

Roman type type style with serifs

rotary press a type of printing press in which the plate is wrapped around a cylinder

rough a preliminary drawing of a layout

routing the distribution of various parts of a form

rule a printed line

rule weight the thickness of the printed line, measured in points

running charge the part of a form's price based upon the press operations, as compared with the one-time or flat charges for makeready

safety paper paper, used primarily for checks, that has been coated so that any attempts at alteration will be highlighted

salesbook group of forms bound in a book, usually with a cover and a stapled stub

sans serif a type style without serifs—the flourishes at the ends of letter segments

score an indentation on a sheet to assist in folding

screen a uniform pattern of dots that creates a shading effect on the printed form; the extent of the ink coverage indicated by a percentage figure

sectional fastening a fastening technique for continuous forms that fastens different portions of the forms set in different ways for different usage requirements

selective imaging a type of forms construction that provides different imaging on the various parts; done with patterned carbons, printed blockouts, desensitized or sensitized carbonless papers

self-checking number *see* check digit

self-contained carbonless chemical carbonless paper with both the "front" and "back" chemicals either in or on the same sheet, eliminating the need for two sheets to form an image

sensitize to coat a sheet with the carbonless chemical, either fully or in any desired pattern, to provide the most effective selective imaging capability

serif the short marks at the end of every character element in Roman typefaces

set a form consisting of more than one part

setup charge *see* flat charge

shading various tones of a color on a form, produced by screening

shelf life the length of time during which a form will perform properly, especially applied to carbon papers, stencils, and masters

shift space the area within which a window envelope insert will shift inside the envelope

shingled a way of using or displaying forms where the edge of each form extends beyond the form above

short carbon carbon paper in unit sets that is shorter than the paper; provides a pull-out margin

show through when the material printed on the back can be seen on the front of the form

side heading a layout technique where main headings are on the side of a zone rather than on top; it saves vertical space on the form

side stub a unit set with the stub on the side, usually on the left, instead of at the top or bottom

single a one-part form, either cut or continuous

skew a deviation from horizontal or vertical, especially important for machine-readable characters

skip perforation a perforation that does not run the full length or width of a form

Snap Out a trademark of the Snap Out Forms Co. for its unit-set construction, often improperly used as a generic term

snap perforation a perforation used at the stub of a unit set to allow a clean, easy separation

solid line glue a permanent fastening for forms using a continuous line of glue

source document the form that provides the data for a computer input operation

spacing the intervals between lines or characters; also, the amount of entry space allowed for user data entry

spot carbon *see* patterned carbon

spot glue permanent fastening consisting of dots of glue; provides a more flexible stub than solid line glue

stat commonly used term for a photocopy (short for Photostat)

stencil a waxy sheet which allows ink to pass through only characters or lines that have been cut through it; used for masters and label preparation

step and repeat a camera process that produces multiple images on a single layout from the same original

stitching stapling

stock form a continuous form, either completely blank or with only evenly spaced horizontal lines; used for production of many different output reports

strike-off a test run of a dummy form

strike-on image camera copy produced by a typewriter-like composer

strip, stripping putting the negative or negatives into a masking sheet to prepare the copy for photographing

strip carbon carbon paper with uncoated areas running parallel with the marginal strips

stub the fastened portion of a set, usually glued

stub dimension the length of the stub on a unit set

stub roll *see* butt roll

substance *see* basis weight

tab on typewriters, horizontal space passed over by a skipping carriage motion, to speed typing and to simplify typing in columns

tab card the card used as input to a computer; printed on 99# tab-card stock; usually has one corner cut off; the standard size is 7⅜″ × 3¼″

tab form a continuous form

tag a strong grade of heavy paper used where strength, thickness, and durability are important

temporary fastenings fastenings, such as crimps and fugitive glue, for continuous forms

tenting a problem with continuous forms when the perforated folds do not fully conform to the platen

thermography a printing method where an ink and powder are applied to the paper and then baked, giving a raised image like engraving

three-ring punch the hole punch commonly used on the 11″ side of an 8½″ × 11″ sheet for use in a binder; the holes are ¼″ in diameter and 4¼″ from center to center, with the inside of the holes ½″ from the edge of the paper

throw the line spacing of writing equipment—for example, a normal typewriter's throw is six lines per inch

ties per inch the number of uncut areas in 1″ of a perforated line

tight perforation a perforation that is hard to tear

timing mark a character or symbol on a scanning form that tells the machine where to start reading

tint a general, overall shading of a form using a very light screen; used to color code parts when all plies are printed on white paper

tip on to attach one piece of paper to another with glue; implies a manual operation as compared with glueing on a collator

tissue the paper used as the base for carbon paper

t l r b top, left, right, bottom of sheet

torn size   the size of the form after the stub has been removed

tractor   the pinfeed device that moves the form through a printer or other equipment

transfer letters   type that can be transferred from a plastic sheet to a piece of paper by using pressure; normally used only for relatively large characters because of the slow process

tumblehead   *see* head-to-foot

type   a character in a form that allows it to be used to prepare camera-ready copy for printing

typefaces   styles of type (about 2,000 now in existence)

typing carbon   carbon paper designed to transfer an image most effectively upon impact, rather than through a gliding impression made by writing; usually produced in black

ULC design   upper left caption technique of forms layout (*also called* box design)

underrun   that amount less than the quantity ordered; printing industry trade practices provide for an allowance of 10 percent less than the ordered quantity (*see also* overrun)

unit set   two or more sheets held together for use as a single entity for part of their processing, with carbon paper included between the plies unless made of carbonless paper

____ -up   the number of images of the form printed on a single sheet or press revolution, such as two-up, three-up, and so on

upcharge   portions of the form's selling price for special features such as premium papers, special holes, fastenings, inks, numbering, and so on

uppercase letters   capital letters

vellum   transluscent paper commonly used for engineering-type drawings and documents

vertical perforation   a perforation running up and down the form

washup   the press operation required between the application of different ink colors

web   a roll of paper used for printing

web direction   fibers of paper run parallel with the long dimension of the roll (*see also* grain direction)

web-fed press   a rotary press fed by a roll of paper rather than sheets

width   the horizontal dimension of a form as it is used

wire side   the back side of a sheet of paper—the side in contact with the screen on the paper machine during production

write-through   the situation of an image transferring through more than one unit set at a time, especially in book constructions

Xerox   a trademark, as well as a corporate name, often incorrectly used as a generic term for a copy or a copy process

INDEX

Boldface type refers to pages showing forms or examples.